JULIUS CAESAR

WILLIAM SHAKESPEARE

JULIUS CAESAR

With Contemporary Criticism

Edited by JOSEPH PEARCE

IGNATIUS PRESS   SAN FRANCISCO

Cover art:
The Assassination of Caesar
Friedrich Heinrich Füger (1751–1818)

Photo Credit: Nimatallah/Art Resource, N.Y.

Cover design by John Herreid

©2012 by Ignatius Press, San Francisco
ISBN 978-1-58617-616-7
Library of Congress Control Number 2011940711
Printed in Italy ∞

Tradition is the extension of Democracy through time; it is the proxy of the dead and the enfranchisement of the unborn.

Tradition may be defined as the extension of the franchise. Tradition means giving votes to the most obscure of all classes, our ancestors. It is the democracy of the dead. Tradition refuses to submit to the small and arrogant oligarchy of those who merely happen to be walking about. All democrats object to men being disqualified by the accident of birth; tradition objects to their being disqualified by the accident of death. Democracy tells us not to neglect a good man's opinion, even if he is our groom; tradition asks us not to neglect a good man's opinion, even if he is our father. I, at any rate, cannot separate the two ideas of democracy and tradition.

—G. K. Chesterton

Ignatius Critical Editions—Tradition-Oriented Criticism for a new generation

CONTENTS

INTRODUCTION

Joseph Pearce
Ave Maria University

Julius Caesar is one of the most popular of Shakespeare's plays and is on more high school curricula than any other of the Bard's works, with the possible exception of *Hamlet* or *Romeo and Juliet*. Such popularity, from a literary standpoint, is a little difficult to fathom. The play does not plumb the depths of the human condition in the manner of *Hamlet, Macbeth, King Lear,* or *Othello*, nor does it soar to the heights of virtue in its depiction of heroes or heroines. Indeed, it could be argued, and has been argued, that the play lacks a hero of any sort. Its principal characters pale into relative insignificance and seem almost superficial in the company of the prince of Denmark or the thane of Cawdor. Shakespeare's Caesar, in the full pomp of his power, lacks the kingly majesty of Lear, which the latter retains even in the full degradation of his madness; Caesar's ghost is a pretty insubstantial waif beside the formidable presence of the Ghost of Hamlet's father; Shakespeare's Brutus is a far less convincing idealist, even when adhering stoically to his ideals, than is Timon of Athens in his embittered disillusionment with his; and Shakespeare's Cassius is a pretty poor excuse for a cynically manipulative Machiavel when compared to Iago, King Claudius, or either of the diabolical Macbeths. Nor does *Julius Caesar* boast a powerful feminine presence, which is such a vital force, for good or ill, in many of Shakespeare's greatest plays. There is no *femme formidable* to imbue the drama with a feminine touch of sanity and sanctity. There is no Cordelia to prick the conscience of the king; no Isabella to tower over venality with moral rectitude; no Miranda to mirror the beauty and wonder of innocence; no Ophelia, whose very weakness exudes a powerful presence; no Desdemona, whose constancy marks her as a martyr for love. At the other end of the Bard's feminine spectrum, there are no *femmes fatales* whose very presence adds not only spice but poison to the Bard's simmering plots. There is no Didoesquely destructive Cleopatra; no demonically deadly Lady Macbeth; no treacherous Regan or Goneril. Instead, we are offered only two marginal and marginalized female characters, Calphurnia and Portia, whose presence is so sylph-like that we can almost forget that they are there. Calphurnia, Caesar's wife, is so insubstantial that she is cast aside by her husband with almost careless indifference. How different she is from the domineering Lady Macbeth, who brushes her husband's misgivings to one side with browbeating brusqueness. Similarly, Portia, Brutus' wife, is brushed aside by her husband, in spite of her entreaties. Her death offstage, lacking the potency or the pathos of Ophelia's offstage death, is almost shrugged off as a seeming irrelevance or as a distraction from more important things. How different she is from Shakespeare's other Portia, the indomitable heroine of *The Merchant of Venice*, whose eloquence is perhaps unmatched anywhere else in Shakespeare's oeuvre.

Considering its relatively lightweight character, one wonders why *Julius Caesar* remains so enduringly popular. Leonard F. Dixon, pondering this question in 1968, attributed it to extraliterary factors:

> Because of its use in the schools, *Julius Caesar* is one of the best known of Shakespeare's plays, and yet it has not generally been talked about as a play. It probably got into the curriculum to begin with for institutional rather than dramatic reasons: the best possible English substitute for Latin, gives practice in public speaking, not sexy, easily cast in a boys' school, and so on. It apparently meant a great deal to nineteenth-century critics, but they thought of it not so much as a play as a collection of biographies, particularly of Brutus, an aristocrat whom they could praise and patronize at the same time.[1]

---

[1] Leonard F. Dean, ed., *Twentieth Century Interpretations of "Julius Caesar"* (Englewood Cliffs, N.J.: Prentice-Hall, 1968), p. 1.

Dixon's comments, written almost half a century ago, seem a trifle dated. Very few schools continue to teach Latin, removing the need to seek substitutes for it. The study of rhetoric is similarly no longer on high school curricula, so the play's rhetorically charged funeral orations are no longer valued for the practice they offer in public speaking. In a sexualized culture that has taken to reading *Romeo and Juliet* with the same breathless abandonment of reason that characterizes the play's "star-cross'd lovers", *Julius Caesar*'s not being "sexy" is no longer an attribute but a liability. The triumph of coeducation has threatened single-sex schools with extinction, so the fact that the almost complete absence of female characters made *Julius Caesar* "easily cast in a boys' school" is of negligible relevance in today's educational culture.

Pace Dixon, *Julius Caesar* retains its popularity because it allows the designers of high school curricula to kill two birds with one stone. It serves not merely as literature but as history, enabling schools to teach Shakespeare and Roman history simultaneously. Like the nineteenth-century critics to whom Dixon alludes, twenty-first-century teachers are often more concerned with *Julius Caesar* "not so much as a play as a collection of biographies". To the extent that the life of Caesar and the circumstances surrounding his assassination continue to fascinate the imagination, it is scarcely surprising that a dramatic representation of one of the most famous chapters in human history by human history's most famous playwright is perennially popular.

Long before Shakespeare wrote his version, the story of Caesar's assassination had fascinated Elizabethan playgoers. As early as 1562, two years before Shakespeare's birth, the diarist Henry Machyn referred to his seeing a dramatic performance of a play about Caesar. In 1594, as Shakespeare was establishing his own reputation as a playwright, the theater owner Philip Henslowe recorded in his diary that his theater company performed a two-part play about Caesar. Shakespeare must have been familiar with this play, and we can only conjecture the extent to which his own play, written some five years later, was a response to this earlier version.

All the evidence suggests that Shakespeare's *Caesar* was premiered sometime in 1599. Thomas Platter, visiting London from Basle in Switzerland, noted that he had seen a play, *Vom ersten Keyser* (The first Caesar), on September 21, 1599, in a theater on the south side of the Thames. Platter's dating of the play is confirmed by the writer John Weever, who refers to *Julius Caesar* in one of his own books, written in 1599.[2] Since Francis Meres does not list *Caesar* in the list of Shakespeare's plays in his *Palladis Tamia*, published in the autumn of 1598, it seems safe to date the play with some precision.

Since Shakespeare's modus operandi often involved the confuting of his sources, correcting their biases and changing them into modes of expression more conducive to his own beliefs, it is possible that his own *Caesar* was a response to, or a reaction against, the earlier version produced by Henslowe's company. Shakespeare had written his play *King John* as a reaction against the anti-Catholic bias of an earlier play entitled *The Troublesome Reign of King John*. Similarly, his inspiration for *Romeo and Juliet* was Arthur Brooke's long poem *The Tragicall Historye of Romeus and Juliet*, published in 1562, which had cast the friar in the role of the villain. Shakespeare wrote *Hamlet* in response to an earlier play, which scholars now call the *Ur-Hamlet*, that was probably written by Thomas Kyd. Although Kyd's play has been lost to posterity, the fact that Kyd had been tried and imprisoned for atheism in 1593 suggests that Shakespeare had sought to "baptize" the story of Hamlet with his own profoundly Christian imagination. This revisiting of older works to correct their defects was employed once again in the writing of *King Lear*, in which Shakespeare clearly intended to counter the anti-Catholic bias of an earlier play, *The True Chronicle History of King Leir and his three daughters*, which was probably written by George Peele. Similarly, Shakespeare seems to have written *Macbeth* to comment

---

[2] The reference appears in Weever's *The Mirror of Martyrs, or The Life and Death of Sir John Oldcastle*. Although this was not published until 1601, Weever writes that it was "ready for the Press some two years ago"; i.e., it was written in 1599.

upon an earlier play on a similar theme, *The Tragedy of Gow-rie*, which had been banned, presumably by direct order of the king himself. Since this process of creative revisionism (to give it a name) seems part of Shakespeare's inspirational motivation in selecting a theme upon which to write, it would seem reasonable to suspect that Shakespeare's *Caesar* was, in some sense, a reaction to the earlier play performed by Henslowe's company. Since Henslowe's *Caesar* has not survived, its importance as a source for Shakespeare's play will remain a mystery. Its importance is not, however, diminished by the mystery. Much of what is really important to history has been lost to posterity yet remains a real presence in spite of its apparent absence. In this particular case, it is likely that we would know more about Shakespeare's play if we had access to Henslowe's. Although such access is denied, we have a better perspective of the overall picture from our under-standing that the missing pieces of the puzzle are nonetheless important.

Other possible sources for Shakespeare's *Caesar* include Rob-ert Garnier's *Cornélie*, translated into English by Thomas Kyd; the translation was published in 1594, five years before Shake-speare began work on his own play. In Garnier's five-act play, Caesar is very much the villain whose arrogance and wicked ambition bring about the destruction of all that is noble in the Roman Republic. Although Shakespeare must have known Kyd's translation, and although it is customary for critics to see parallels between Garnier's Caesar and Shakespeare's, it is perilous to see them too synonymously. Shakespeare's Caesar is certainly arrogant, but his ambition is treated somewhat ambivalently, so much so that it is almost eclipsed by the ambi-tion of his enemies, particularly that of Cassius but, to a lesser extent, of Brutus also. Clearly, Shakespeare's perspective can-not be simplistically conflated with the anti-Caesarean tradi-tion of sixteenth-century French drama. This being so, Shakespeare's begging to differ with the anti-Caesarean approach of Garnier and, by extension, with similar plays by earlier French writers, such as Marc-Antoine Muret and Jacques

Grévin, suggests that he is uncomfortable with their enthusiasm for Caesar's assassins.

It would, of course, be a sin of omission to fail to mention Plutarch in a discussion of Shakespeare's sources for *Julius Caesar*. Plutarch's *Lives*, which contained biographical studies of Caesar, Brutus, and Antony, was written at the beginning of the second century. It would have been available to Shakespeare in Sir Thomas North's translation, published in 1579, and this is commonly assumed to have been the principal source for the play. Such a supposition, though perhaps justified, overlooks the fact that Shakespeare was moving in dramatic circles and that in all probability he was moved primarily by what was unfolding on the Elizabethan stage. Thus, and as we have discussed already, his version of *Caesar* is probably indebted to the unknown play performed by Henslowe's company, to Kyd's translation of Garnier, and even, perhaps, to another anonymous play, *Caesar's Revenge*, which was not registered until 1606 but is believed to have antedated Shakespeare's play. Ultimately, Plutarch's seminal work deserves pride of place, not so much for its direct influence on Shakespeare, however pronounced and profound it might be, but for its role as the taproot from which all these various dramatizations stemmed. Nonetheless, it is likely that Shakespeare consulted North's translation of Plutarch in his preparation for writing the play, and it is clear that his overarching moral perspective mirrors that of Plutarch. Shakespeare, like Plutarch, represents the people of Rome as fickle and confused and as being easily manipulated by the skillful use—or abuse—of rhetoric. Like Plutarch, Shakespeare depicts Cassius as someone motivated more by personal hatred of Caesar than by any political principles. Also following Plutarch, Shakespeare paints Brutus somewhat sympathetically but as being culpable for his actions, particularly in his allowing himself to be duped by Cassius and in his imprudent and intemperate hastiness in joining the conspiracy. Echoing Plutarch's political reading of events, Shakespeare illustrates that the conspiracy not only fails in its objective to bring liberty and order to Rome but is the harbinger of anarchy, from which a succession of tyrants would emerge. Shakespeare, like Plutarch, is more concerned with moral character than with historical fact, concentrating on the consequences of the good or bad motives and choices of the human person. As with Plutarch, Shakespeare uses history to teach perennial lessons about the nature of man.

It is necessary to study the play's four main characters more closely to discover the extent to which Shakespeare's play is as moralistic, in the good sense of the word, and as ethically judicious as Plutarch's *Lives*. Since such a study is not possible within the constraints imposed by the space allotted to an introduction, and since there are already excellent essays on Brutus and Cassius elsewhere in this edition, we will concentrate our attention on the play's eponymous character and its alleged "hero".

When we approach Shakespeare's Caesar, we are shocked by the discrepancy between the enormous presence of the public persona and the pathetic reality of the private man. On the one hand, Caesar is the most powerful man in the Western world; on the other, he is prone to physical maladies and is seen to be both physically and morally weak. This anomalous abyss separating the image from the reality is present in the very form of the play. While Caesar is the eponymous hero of the whole drama, the star of the show, whose name appears in lights as the one who lends his name to the play's title, he is only a peripheral character, brushed aside by Brutus as contemptuously as Caesar brushes aside the protestations of his wife. Compared to Brutus and Cassius, he has a minor role, even in his own play, and it is ironic that his power resides not in the vacuous nature of his words but in the vacuum created by his absence. Caesar's lines in the play are among the least memorable, especially when compared to the funeral orations of Brutus or Antony, or the Machiavellian asides of Cassius. Furthermore, his relatively few lines serve to highlight his lack of judgment and his hypocrisy. Almost the first thing he does is ignore the warnings of the Soothsayer that he should "[b]eware the ides of March" (1.2.18, 23).[3] Dismissing the true prophet of his own impending doom as "a dreamer", he exits immediately afterward, with all his entourage, leaving only Brutus and Cassius on stage. Thus, within moments of Caesar's impetuous dismissal of the words of the prophet, we see Cassius poisoning the ear of Brutus, thereby laying the foundations for the assassination that the Soothsayer had prophesied.

When we next see Caesar, he is expressing his distrust of Cassius to Antony:

Caesar. Let me have men about me that are fat;
   Sleek-headed men, and such as sleep o' nights.
   Yond Cassius has a lean and hungry look;
   He thinks too much. Such men are dangerous.

Antony. Fear him not, Caesar, he's not dangerous;
   He is a noble Roman, and well given.

Caesar. Would he were fatter! But I fear him not.
   Yet if my name were liable to fear,
   I do not know the man I should avoid
   So soon as that spare Cassius. He reads much,
   He is a great observer, and he looks
   Quite through the deeds of men. He loves no plays,
   As thou dost, Antony; he hears no music.
   Seldom he smiles, and smiles in such a sort
   As if he mock'd himself, and scorn'd his spirit
   That could be mov'd to smile at anything.
   Such men as he be never at heart's ease
   Whiles they behold a greater than themselves,
   And therefore are they very dangerous.
   I rather tell thee what is to be fear'd
   Than what I fear; for always I am Caesar.
   Come on my right hand, for this ear is deaf,
   And tell me truly what thou think'st of him. (1.2.192–214)

[3] All quotations from *Julius Caesar* are from the edition published by Ignatius Press: *Julius Caesar*, ed. Joseph Pearce, Ignatius Critical Editions (San Francisco: Ignatius Press, 2012).

Here we see Caesar at his most prescient but also at his most preposterous. We know that he is right to mistrust Cassius because we have just witnessed Cassius in the seditious act of tempting Brutus. Yet he refuses to act upon his private fears because his artificially constructed public persona must appear to be fearless. Caesar, the self-deified ruler of the known world, does not know fear. As with his dismissal of the Soothsayer, his dismissal of his justifiable fears about Cassius show that Caesar's idolization of himself, his deification of the figment of himself that he has created, cushions him from any sensibility of the real mortal danger that he is facing.

Embedded within this speech is a metadramatic reference to the turbulent politics of Shakespeare's own day. Caesar's reference to Cassius as one who is not to be trusted because "[h]e loves no plays" and "hears no music" is clearly an attack on the Puritans in Elizabethan England, who considered the theater and dancing to be sinful and who were against the use of polyphony or chant in the liturgy. Caesar's words are a reiteration of the words of Lorenzo in the final act of *The Merchant of Venice*, which Shakespeare had written three or four years earlier:

> The man that hath no music in himself,
> Nor is not moved with concord of sweet sounds,
> Is fit for treasons, stratagems, and spoils;
> The motions of his spirit are dull as night,
> And his affections dark as [Erebus]:
> Let no such man be trusted. Mark the music.[4]

As is so often the case in Shakespeare's plays, his villain is tagged by these topical references as both a Machiavellian and a Puritan, reminding us that Shakespeare was always writing with his own turbulent time in mind, even when his theme is ostensibly the distant past or distant countries. We should remind ourselves that political and religious censorship prevailed

---

[4] *The Merchant of Venice*, ed. Joseph Pearce, Ignatius Critical Editions (San Francisco: Ignatius Press, 2009), 5.1.83–88.

in Elizabethan England, so that it was impossible for a playwright to write openly about political and religious issues. In choosing to set his plays in the past or in foreign countries, such as Italy, he could give his plays a convivial Catholic setting without incurring the wrath of the censors. Even then, an element of circumspection and due decorum was essential. At the very time that Shakespeare was writing *Julius Caesar*, the Anglican church, in what became known as the Bishops' Ban, was seeking to suppress dissident and dissenting voices on the stage. On June 1, 1599, the archbishop of Canterbury, John Whitgift, and the bishop of London, Richard Bancroft, issued a ban on certain works and ordered that no further English history plays be printed unless approved by the queen's Privy Council, that is, the government. It is notable, for instance, that Shakespeare wrote no further English history plays after this ban was imposed, suggesting that his own work was considered suspect by the authorities.[5] Thereafter, he often chose ancient Rome as the historical settings for his plays, circumventing the ban. This may also have been the reason that Shakespeare chose to write on Caesar at this particular time and not earlier.

The next time we see Caesar is in Act 2, when his wife, Calphurnia, is endeavoring to dissuade him from going to the Senate. She had been beset with nightmares during the previous night, in which she had seen visions of her husband being murdered. She is further troubled by reports of "horrid sights" (2.2.16) throughout the city during the previous night's storm, corroborating the stories recounted by Casca and Cinna at the end of Act 1. As with the horrors of the storm in *Macbeth*, Shakespeare evokes the way that natural and supernatural forces roar in outrage at the foul deeds of sinful men, and, as with the vision of the Ghost at the beginning of *Hamlet*, he is at pains to cite several independent witnesses to establish the objectivity and authenticity of the visions, precluding

---

[5] Although *Henry VIII* is believed to be by Shakespeare, at least in part, it does not seem to have been written until 1612 or 1613, after Shakespeare had retired to Stratford, many years after the ban, and several years after Whitgift's and Bancroft's deaths.

the possibility of explaining the portents away as mere hallucinations. Once again, as with the case of the Soothsayer, Caesar has been given ample warning of the mortal danger in which he finds himself, and once again he dismisses the warnings. When the augurers, having made sacrifice to the gods, confirm Calphurnia's fears, adding their voice to hers in advising Caesar not to venture forth from his home because of the portents of doom they have received, he remains dismissively aloof:

> Caesar should be a beast without a heart,
> If he should stay at home to-day for fear.
> No, Caesar shall not. Danger knows full well
> That Caesar is more dangerous than he:
> We are two lions litter'd in one day,
> And I the elder and more terrible;
> And Caesar shall go forth. (2.2.42–48)

Although Caesar's defiance of death exhibits the outward markings of commendable courage, he is betrayed by his false vision of himself. Caesar does not need to fear danger because Caesar is more dangerous than fear itself. He is older and more terrible than fear. This self-deification is not merely pompous but also pathetic. As we watch Caesar put himself upon an Olympian pedestal, we do not know whether to laugh or cry. Indeed, the whole scene descends from pathos to bathos when Caesar is ultimately duped into believing that all the omens were good portents by the deliberate deception of one of the conspirators, Decius Brutus, who had earlier boasted that he could manipulate Caesar and make him do his will through the use of flattery. The irony is that the mighty Caesar, who likens himself to a god, is in fact nothing more than one of the "gilded butterflies" that the wizened Lear laughs at in his hard-earned wisdom. Caesar, for all his supercilious grandiloquence, flutters to his death on the wings of flattery.

En route to the Capitol, Caesar is met once again by the persistent Soothsayer, who repeats his warning, and also by Artemidorus, a teacher of rhetoric, who endeavors to give

Caesar a note warning him of the conspiracy. Both men are dismissed with blithe indifference as Caesar proceeds with impregnable ignorance to his doom. His final moments are pregnant with irony as he boasts that he will not succumb to flattery, which he describes as the "sweet words,/Low-crooked curtsies, and base spaniel fawning" that "[melt] fools" (3.1.42–43). Considering that he has just been fooled by flattery, a flattery that will fell him fatally, he is, by his own definition, a fool whose life is about to melt away in the heat of its own folly. His last speech is full of pomposity and arrogance, culminating in one final bombastic act of hubris, in which he likens his immutable will to that of "Olympus", before he is cut down (3.1.73). The final irony and the final Shakespearean insult to Caesar's majesty reside in the fact that his final words, his most famous, point not to his own majesty but to the triumph of his nemesis: "Et tu, Brute?—Then fall, Caesar!" As Caesar falls from his self-constructed and misconstructed Olympus, the enormity of his fall is dwarfed by the enormity of Brutus' treachery.

Although Shakespeare's Caesar is a somewhat pathetic figure, it is a grievous misreading of the play to see his assassination as justifiable or even praiseworthy. Cassius, the progenitor of the plot to kill Caesar, is clearly the play's overarching villain. Motivated by hatred and envy and prone to corruption, Cassius is cast in the role of the Machiavel, the cynical manipulator who appears in many of Shakespeare's plays. He is numbered with Iago, King Claudius, Polonius, Edmund, Richard III, and the Macbeths as one of those without faith or principle who prey upon the virtuous and godly. It is inconceivable that a plot hatched by such a serpent could be seen as justifiable. The villainy of Brutus is by no means as obvious but is nonetheless as real. His high ideals do not excuse his low actions, and he reminds modern readers perhaps of the many deadly idealists who have washed themselves clean, as they see it, in the blood of their victims. We think perhaps of Robespierre and the Great Terror, Lenin and the Gulag Archipelago, or Hitler and the Holocaust. It is also interesting that Brutus is condemned unequivocally as a villain in the only critical judgment of Brutus' character from Shakespeare's own time. The poet John Weever, writing in the very year that *Julius Caesar* was first staged, passes this poetic judgment on the viciousness of Brutus:

> The many-headed multitude were drawne
> By Brutus speach, that Caesar was ambitious,
> When eloquent Mark Antonie had showne
> His vertues, who but Brutus then was vicious?[6]

The most convincing argument against the casting of Brutus as a villain is the final laudatory judgment of him by Antony in the play's final scene:

> This was the noblest Roman of them all.
> All the conspirators save only he
> Did that they did in envy of great Caesar;
> He only in a general honest thought
> And common good to all made one of them.
> His life was gentle; and the elements
> So mix'd in him that Nature might stand up
> And say to all the world, "This was a man!" (5.5.68–75)

There is no doubt that eulogistic lines in this vein, when found at the culmination of Shakespeare's plays, are normally reserved for those who are truly worthy of them. Indeed, as Sophia Mason argues with eloquence in her essay "Brutus in Hell" in this edition, it could be that the melting and mellowing of Brutus' stoically hardened heart in the play's final scenes constitutes a genuine conversion to a Christian concept of charity. Perhaps so. On the other hand, the rhetorical device that Shakespeare employs throughout the play is that of irony. Is it not ironic that these words are spoken by the rhetorically manipulative Antony, whose nobility dissolves with

---

[6] John Weever, *The Mirror of Martyrs, or the Life and Death of Sir John Old-castle*, quoted in *The Reader's Encyclopedia of Shakespeare*, ed. Oscar James Campbell and Edward G. Quinn (New York: MJF Books, 1966), p. 411.

his first bloodlustful taste of real power? Do we believe him? Are we meant to believe him?

In the final analysis, the most striking feature of *Julius Caesar* is that none of its principal characters are particularly virtuous. This is not unique in the Shakespearean canon. We think perhaps of *Romeo and Juliet*, in which none of the characters show much virtue except for the fatally flawed friar. It is, however, unusual to see the absence of virtue to such a striking degree. It is not like the Shakespeare that we know and love. And herein lies another solution to the problem we posed earlier with regard to the secret of the play's popularity in the modern academy. The modern academy is uncomfortable with morality; it has squeezed virtue from the curriculum with its vicelike grip; it has an unhealthy disdain for the healthy. It thrives on moral ambiguity and ambivalence. It is no wonder that it is at home with the apparent moral ambivalence of the characters in *Julius Caesar*. It is also no wonder that it is at home with the high degree of irony with which Shakespeare spices his plot. The sneer of irony is the cynical grin on the face of most modern criticism. It is the only humor with which it is entirely comfortable. It is, therefore, not surprising that the academy is comfortable with *Julius Caesar*, a play that is full of endearing sinners and is not polluted by the grace of sanctity.

And yet are we really meant to believe that the same playwright who wrote so many other plays that are permeated throughout with Christian realism and orthodox Christian theology also wrote a work of nihilistic irony? Evidently, if we are reading the play as the modern critics are reading it, we cannot be reading it as it was written or as it was meant to be performed or read. How, then, should we read it?

As with all literature, the play should be read through the eyes of the author, as far as this is possible, which in Shakespeare's case means reading it through the eyes of an orthodox Christian living in Elizabethan England. When we read the play through these eyes, which are so much more lucid than our own or those of today's hopelessly wayward critics, we see the same profound morality emerging that we see in his other works. On the most obvious level, Shakespeare is echoing the words of Mercutio in *Romeo and Juliet*. He is calling down a plague on all their houses, in the sense that he is pouring scorn on Caesar's vanity, on Antony's bloodthirsty opportunism, on Cassius' ambition, on Brutus' brutal idealism. Yet, unlike Mercutio, he is not cursing from the perspective of a worldly cynic but from that of a believing Christian at a time when believing Christians were being tortured and put to death by the vanity of monarchs, by bloodthirsty opportunists, by political ambition, and by brutal idealism.

There is, however, a deeper level of meaning that is all too often overlooked completely. It is the sound of silence within the play; the scream in a vacuum; the unheard and unheeded voice of the virtuous. It is the voice of Calphurnia, which, if heeded, would have saved Caesar's life; it is the voice of Portia, which, if heeded, might have urged Brutus to think twice about his involvement with the conspirators. It is the voice of the Soothsayer and of the augurers. It is the voice of Artemidorus, a teacher of rhetoric, whose note to Caesar is devoid of all rhetorical devices and direct to the point of bluntness:

> Caesar, beware of Brutus; take heed of Cassius; come not near Casca; have an eye to Cinna; trust not Trebonius; mark well Metellus Cimber; Decius Brutus loves thee not; thou hast wrong'd Caius Ligarius. There is but one mind in all these men, and it is bent against Caesar. If thou beest not immortal, look about you. Security gives way to conspiracy. The mighty gods defend thee! (2.3.1–6)

The note is not read, the voice is not heard, and the consequences are fatal.

All that was missing in the play is the one thing necessary, the still, small voice of calm that the proud refuse to hear.

TEXTUAL NOTE

This edition of *Julius Caesar* follows the First Folio of 1623, the only authoritative text of the play. No edition of the play was published prior to the First Folio, and no quarto editions were published until the latter half of the seventeenth century.

The Text of

JULIUS CAESAR

DRAMATIS PERSONAE

Julius Caesar
Octavius Caesar ⎫
Marcus Antonius ⎬ triumvirs[1] after the death of Julius
M. Aemil. Lepidus ⎭ Caesar
Cicero ⎫
Publius ⎬ senators[2]
Popilius Lena ⎭
Marcus Brutus ⎫
Cassius ⎪
Casca ⎪
Trebonius ⎪
Ligarius ⎬ conspirators against Julius Caesar
Decius Brutus ⎪
Metellus Cimber ⎭
Cinna
Flavius ⎫
Marullus ⎬ tribunes[3]
Artemidorus, a sophist[4] of Cnidos[5]
A Soothsayer[6]
Cinna, a poet
Another Poet

---

[1] *triumvirs*: A triumvirate is a form of government headed by three men (triumvirs, or triumviri).

[2] *senators*: The Roman Senate was a "council of elders", a deliberative body that played a vital role in the governance of the Roman Republic.

[3] *tribunes*: elected officials of the Roman Republic.

[4] *sophist*: teacher of rhetoric and philosophy, renowned for powers of adroit reasoning.

[5] *Cnidos*: ancient city of Asia Minor (between the Aegean and the Mediterranean, in present-day Turkey).

[6] *Soothsayer*: man who professes to be able to foretell events by a divinely given power.

Lucilius
Titinius
Messala } friends to Brutus and Cassius
Young Cato
Volumnius
Varro
Clitus
Claudius } servants to Brutus
Strato
Lucius
Dardanius
Pindarus, servant to Cassius
Calphurnia, wife to Caesar
Portia, wife to Brutus
Senators, Citizens, Guards, and Attendants, etc.

4

The Scene: Rome;[7] near Sardis;[8]
near Philippi.[9]

ACT 1

Scene 1. *Rome. A street.*

Enter Flavius, Marullus, and certain Commoners[10] over the stage.

Flavius. Hence![11] home, you idle creatures, get
    you home.
  Is this a holiday? What! know you not,
  Being mechanical,[12] you ought not walk
  Upon a labouring day[13] without the sign
  Of your profession?[14] Speak, what trade art thou?   5

1 Citizen. Why, sir, a carpenter.[15]

Marullus. Where is thy leather apron and thy
    rule?
  What dost thou with thy best apparel on?
  You, sir, what trade are you?

2 Citizen. Truly, sir, in respect of[16] a fine   10
  workman, I am but, as you would say, a cobbler.[17]

Marullus. But what trade art thou? Answer me
    directly.[18]

----

[7] *Rome*: capital of the Roman Empire.

[8] *Sardis*: ancient city in Asia Minor.

[9] *Philippi*: town in eastern Macedonia.

[10] *Commoners*: plebeians (usually sympathetic to a monarchy).

[11] *Hence!* Go from here!

[12] *mechanical*: description for artisans, people of the working class.

[13] *labouring day*: workday.

[14] *sign / Of your profession*: i.e., working clothes indicative of a given occupation.

[15] *carpenter*: laborer who works with wood (not a joiner, who was specifically a cabinetmaker).

[16] *in respect of*: in comparison to.

[17] *cobbler*: (1) maker and mender of shoes; (2) clumsy bungler.

[18] *directly*: immediately, plainly.

2 Citizen. A trade, sir, that I hope I may use[19] with
a safe conscience, which is indeed, sir, a mender
of bad soles.[20]

Marullus. What trade, thou knave? Thou
naughty[21] knave, what trade?   15

2 Citizen. Nay, I beseech you, sir, be not out[22] with
me; yet, if you be out,[23] sir, I can mend you.[24]

Marullus. What mean'st thou by that? Mend
me, thou saucy[25] fellow!

2 Citizen. Why, sir, cobble you.   20

Flavius. Thou art a cobbler, art thou?

2 Citizen. Truly, sir, all that I live by is with the
awl.[26] I meddle with no tradesman's matters nor
women's matters,[27] but with awl.[28] I am indeed, sir,
a surgeon to old shoes. When they are in great
danger, I re-cover[29] them. As proper[30] men as ever 25
trod upon neat's leather[31] have gone upon my
handiwork.

Flavius. But wherefore art not in thy shop to-
          day?
     Why dost thou lead these men about the
          streets?

[19] *use*: practice.
[20] *soles*: i.e., of shoes (with a pun on "souls").
[21] *naughty*: profligate, ne'er-do-well.
[22] *out*: out of temper, out of humor.
[23] *out*: out of your shoe (i.e., developing a hole).
[24] *mend you*: i.e., (1) mend your worn-out shoe; (2) mend your mood or character.
[25] *saucy*: bold, insolent.
[26] *awl*: pointed tool used in shoemaking.
[27] *women's matters*: a ribald pun.
[28] *with awl*: a pun on "withal", meaning "nevertheless", and "with all".
[29] *re-cover*: (1) repair; (2) restore to health and safety.
[30] *proper*: good.
[31] *neat's leather*: i.e., cowhide.

2 Citizen. Truly, sir, to wear out their shoes, to   30
   get myself into more work. But indeed, sir, we
   make holiday to see Caesar, and to rejoice in his
   triumph.[32]

Marullus. Wherefore rejoice? What conquest
      brings he home?
   What tributaries[33] follow him to Rome,
   To grace in captive bonds his chariot wheels?[34]   35
   You blocks, you stones, you worse than
      senseless things!
   O you hard hearts, you cruel men of Rome,
   Knew you not Pompey?[35] Many a time and oft[36]
   Have you climb'd up to walls and battlements,
   To tow'rs and windows, yea, to chimney-tops,   40
   Your infants in your arms, and there have sat
   The livelong[37] day, with patient expectation,
   To see great Pompey pass the streets of Rome.
   And when you saw his chariot but appear,
   Have you not made an universal shout,   45
   That Tiber trembled underneath her banks,
   To hear the replication[38] of your sounds
   Made in her concave[39] shores?
   And do you now put on your best attire?
   And do you now cull out[40] a holiday?   50
   And do you now strew flowers in his way

---

[32] *triumph*: (1) triumphal procession; (2) military victory.

[33] *tributaries*: captives, who pay tribute money to their conqueror.

[34] *To grace in captive bonds his chariot wheels*: Tributaries were traditionally chained to the chariot wheels of the triumphant warrior.

[35] *Pompey*: Gnaeus Pompeius (106–48 B.C.), also known as Pompey the Great, a military and political leader of the Roman Republic, an ally of Caesar and later his competitor. Pompey's assassination paved the way for Julius Caesar's growth in power.

[36] *oft*: often.

[37] *livelong*: whole.

[38] *replication*: echo, repetition.

[39] *concave*: hollowed out, curved.

[40] *cull out*: collect, select.

That comes in triumph over Pompey's blood?[41]
Be gone!
Run to your houses, fall upon your knees,
Pray to the gods to intermit[42] the plague   55
That needs must light on this ingratitude.

Flavius. Go, go, good countrymen, and for this
    fault
Assemble all the poor men of your sort;[43]
Draw them to Tiber banks,[44] and weep your tears
Into the channel, till the lowest stream   60
Do kiss the most exalted shores of all.[45]

                    [*Exeunt all the Commoners.*]

See whe'r[46] their basest mettle[47] be not mov'd;
They vanish tongue-tied in their guiltiness.
Go you down that way towards the Capitol;[48]
This way will I. Disrobe the images[49]   65
If you do find them deck'd with ceremonies.[50]

Marullus. May we do so?
    You know it is the feast of Lupercal.[51]

[41] *Pompey's blood*: i.e., his sons.

[42] *intermit*: suspend or stop for a time.

[43] *sort*: rank.

[44] *Tiber banks*: Rome was built on the eastern banks of the Tiber River, one of the longest rivers in Italy.

[45] *till the lowest stream . . . exalted shores of all*: i.e., until the water level rises up to the highest water mark.

[46] *whe'r*: whether.

[47] *mettle*: (1) substance; (2) disposition.

[48] *the Capitol*: Capitoline Hill, one of the seven hills of Rome, site of a temple to Jupiter where triumphs were celebrated.

[49] *Disrobe the images*: The commoners have been crowning and dressing the statues as if in ceremonial robes.

[50] *ceremonies*: ceremonial robes.

[51] *Lupercal*: Lupercalia, a fertility festival celebrated February 15. Caesar's triumph actually took place in October 45 B.C. but here is set in February 44 B.C., accelerating the historical time line. This is one of the dramatic changes introduced by Shakespeare to his primary source, the writings of the Greek historian Plutarch (c. 120–46 B.C.).

Flavius. It is no matter; let no images
  Be hung with Caesar's trophies. I'll about,   70
  And drive away the vulgar⁵² from the streets;
  So do you too, where you perceive them thick.
  These growing feathers pluck'd from Caesar's
    wing
  Will make him fly an ordinary pitch,⁵³
  Who else would soar above the view of men,   75
  And keep us all in servile fearfulness.   [*Exeunt.*]

Scene 2. *Rome. A public place.*

Music. Enter Caesar; Antony, for the course; Calphurnia,
Portia, Decius, Cicero, Brutus, Cassius, and Casca;
a great crowd following, among them a Soothsayer;
after them, Marullus and Flavius.

Caesar. Calphurnia.

Casca.   Peace, ho! Caesar speaks.

                          [*Music ceases.*]

Caesar. Calphurnia.

Calphurnia. Here, my lord.

Caesar. Stand you directly in Antonius'
    way
  When he doth run his course. Antonius!

Antony. Caesar, my lord.   5

Caesar. Forget not in your speed, Antonius,
  To touch Calphurnia; for our elders say,

⁵² *vulgar:* i.e., vulgar (poor) people.
⁵³ *pitch:* height.

The barren, touched in this holy chase,
Shake off their sterile curse.[54]

Antony.   I shall remember.
  When Caesar says 'Do this', it is perform'd.   *10*

Caesar. Set on, and leave no ceremony out.

                                        [*Music.*]

Soothsayer. Caesar!

Caesar. Ha! Who calls?

Casca. Bid every noise be still. Peace yet again.

                                   [*Music ceases.*]

Caesar. Who is it in the press[55] that calls on me?   *15*
  I hear a tongue, shriller than all the music,
  Cry 'Caesar!' Speak. Caesar is turn'd to hear.

Soothsayer. Beware the ides of March.[56]

Caesar.   What man is that?

Brutus. A soothsayer bids you beware the ides of
  March.

Caesar. Set him before me; let me see his face.   *20*

Cassius. Fellow, come from the throng; look
  upon Caesar.

Caesar. What say'st thou to me now? Speak once
  again.

Soothsayer. Beware the ides of March.

[54] *The barren . . . sterile curse*: It was believed that the touch of young revelers of this festival would cure barren women from the "curse" of sterility.
[55] *press*: press of people, crowd.
[56] *ides of March*: March 15.

Caesar. He is a dreamer; let us leave him.
    Pass.

       [*Sennet.*[57] *Exeunt all but Brutus and Cassius.*]

Cassius. Will you go see the order of the course?[58]   25

Brutus. Not I.

Cassius. I pray you do.

Brutus. I am not gamesome:[59] I do lack some part
  Of that quick spirit[60] that is in Antony.
  Let me not hinder, Cassius, your desires;   30
  I'll leave you.

Cassius. Brutus, I do observe you now of late;
  I have not from your eyes that gentleness
  And show[61] of love as I was wont[62] to have.
  You bear too stubborn and too strange a hand   35
  Over[63] your friend that loves you.

Brutus.   Cassius,
  Be not deceiv'd. If I have veil'd my look,[64]
  I turn the trouble of my countenance
  Merely[65] upon myself. Vexed I am
  Of late with passions of some difference,[66]   40
  Conceptions only proper to myself,[67]

---

[57] *Sennet*: ceremonial flourish of trumpets.
[58] *order of the course*: how the race is progressing.
[59] *gamesome*: merry, sportive.
[60] *quick spirit*: lively, brisk, or responsive nature.
[61] *show*: demonstration.
[62] *was wont*: have tended.
[63] *bear too stubborn . . . a hand/Over*: i.e., behave too haughtily or distantly toward (a metaphor, from horse riding, describing a rough or unfamiliar rider).
[64] *veil'd my look*: i.e., been reserved or withdrawn in my manner.
[65] *Merely*: entirely, completely.
[66] *passions of some difference*: (1) interior emotional conflict; (2) emotions that cause conflict between Brutus and those close to him (e.g., Caesar).
[67] *Conceptions only proper to myself*: ideas that only concern me.

Which give some soil,[68] perhaps, to my
    behaviours;
But let not therefore my good friends be
    griev'd—
Among which number, Cassius, be you one—
Nor construe[69] any further my neglect   45
Than that poor Brutus, with himself at war,
Forgets the shows of love to other men.

Cassius. Then, Brutus, I have much mistook
    your passion,[70]
By means whereof[71] this breast of mine hath
    buried
Thoughts of great value, worthy cogitations.[72]   50
Tell me, good Brutus, can you see your face?

Brutus. No, Cassius; for the eye sees not itself
    But by reflection, by some other things.

Cassius. 'Tis just;[73]
And it is very much lamented, Brutus,   55
That you have no such mirrors as will turn
Your hidden worthiness into your eye,
That you might see your shadow.[74] I have heard,
Where many of the best respect[75] in Rome—
Except immortal Caesar—speaking of Brutus,   60
And groaning underneath this age's yoke,
Have wish'd that noble Brutus had his eyes.[76]

---

[68] *soil*: discoloration.
[69] *construe*: interpret.
[70] *passion*: feelings.
[71] By *means whereof*: because of which.
[72] *cogitations*: thoughts, notions.
[73] *just*: true.
[74] *shadow*: reflection (i.e., his appearance as others perceive him).
[75] *best respect*: highest reputation or regard.
[76] *had his eyes*: i.e., could see himself and the situation as others do.

Brutus. Into what dangers would you lead me,
        Cassius,
    That you would have me seek into myself
    For that which is not in me?   65

Cassius. Therefore, good Brutus, be prepar'd to
        hear;
    And since you know you cannot see yourself
    So well as by reflection, I, your glass,[77]
    Will modestly discover[78] to yourself
    That of yourself which you yet know not of.   70
    And be not jealous on[79] me, gentle[80] Brutus:
    Were I a common laughter,[81] or did use
    To stale with ordinary[82] oaths my love
    To every new protester;[83] if you know
    That I do fawn on[84] men and hug them hard,   75
    And after scandal[85] them; or if you know
    That I profess myself[86] in banqueting
    To all the rout,[87] then hold me dangerous.

                              [*Flourish and shout.*]

Brutus. What means this shouting? I do fear the
        people
    Choose Caesar for their king.

Cassius.   Ay, do you fear it?   80
    Then must I think you would not have it so.

---

[77] *glass:* mirror.
[78] *discover:* reveal.
[79] *jealous on:* distrustful, suspicious of.
[80] *gentle:* noble.
[81] *common laughter:* absurdity, common subject for public laughter.
[82] *ordinary:* commonplace, everyday.
[83] *protester:* someone who too eagerly swears friendship.
[84] *fawn on:* flatter, seek to ingratiate oneself with.
[85] *scandal:* slander.
[86] *profess myself:* i.e., declare myself a friend.
[87] *rout:* rabble, common crowd.

Brutus. I would not, Cassius; yet I love him well.
  But wherefore do you hold me here so long?
  What is it that you would impart to me?
  If it be aught[88] toward the general[89] good,   85
  Set honour in one eye and death i' th' other,
  And I will look on both indifferently;[90]
  For let the gods so speed me[91] as I love
  The name of honour more than I fear death.

Cassius. I know that virtue to be in you, Brutus,   90
  As well as I do know your outward favour.[92]
  Well, honour is the subject of my story.
  I cannot tell what you and other men
  Think of this life; but, for my single self,
  I had as lief[93] not be as live to be   95
  In awe of such a thing as I myself.[94]
  I was born free as Caesar; so were you.
  We both have fed as well, and we can both
  Endure the winter's cold as well as he.
  For once, upon a raw and gusty day,   100
  The troubled Tiber chafing with[95] her shores,
  Caesar said to me 'Dar'st thou, Cassius, now
  Leap in with me into this angry flood,
  And swim to yonder point?' Upon the word,
  Accoutred[96] as I was, I plunged in   105
  And bade him follow. So indeed he did.
  The torrent roar'd, and we did buffet it
  With lusty[97] sinews, throwing it aside

[88] *aught*: anything.
[89] *general*: public.
[90] *indifferently*: impartially, without bias.
[91] *speed me*: prosper me, bless my enterprises.
[92] *favour*: appearance, features, or persona.
[93] *as lief*: just as soon.
[94] *such a thing as I myself*: i.e., another man.
[95] *chafing with*: raging against.
[96] *Accoutred*: fully armed.
[97] *lusty*: powerful, forceful.

And stemming[98] it with hearts of controversy;[99]
But ere we could arrive[100] the point propos'd,   *110*
Caesar cried 'Help me, Cassius, or I sink!'
I, as Aeneas,[101] our great ancestor,
Did from the flames of Troy upon his shoulder
The old Anchises bear, so from the waves of
    Tiber
Did I the tired Caesar. And this man   *115*
Is now become a god; and Cassius is
A wretched creature, and must bend his body
If Caesar carelessly but nod on him.
He had a fever when he was in Spain,
And when the fit was on him I did mark   *120*
How he did shake. 'Tis true, this god did shake.
His coward lips did from their colour fly,[102]
And that same eye, whose bend[103] doth awe the
    world,
Did lose his[104] lustre. I did hear him groan.
Ay, and that tongue of his, that bade the
    Romans   *125*
Mark him, and write his speeches in their
    books,[105]
Alas! it cried 'Give me some drink, Titinius'
As[106] a sick girl. Ye gods! it doth amaze me
A man of such a feeble temper[107] should

---

[98] *stemming*: making headway against.

[99] *hearts of controversy*: hearts eager for the fight.

[100] *arrive*: arrive at.

[101] *Aeneas*: in mythology, a Trojan hero who rescued his father, Anchises, during the sack of Troy and went on through many adventures to found Rome.

[102] *His coward lips did from their colour fly*: The color left his lips like a cowardly soldier would fly—with the "colors" of his banner—from a battle.

[103] *bend*: gaze, stern glance.

[104] *his*: its.

[105] *books*: (1) ancient scrapbooks; (2) historical records.

[106] *As*: like.

[107] *temper*: temperament, constitution.

So get the start of[108] the majestic world,   *130*
And bear the palm[109] alone.   [*Shout. Flourish.*[110]]

Brutus. Another general shout!
   I do believe that these applauses are
   For some new honours that are heap'd on
      Caesar.

Cassius. Why, man, he doth bestride[111] the narrow
      world   *135*
   Like a Colossus,[112] and we petty men
   Walk under his huge legs, and peep about
   To find ourselves dishonourable graves.[113]
   Men at some time are masters of their fates;
   The fault, dear Brutus, is not in our stars,[114]   *140*
   But in ourselves, that we are underlings.
   'Brutus' and 'Caesar'. What should be in that
      'Caesar'?
   Why should that name be sounded[115] more than
      yours?
   Write them together: yours is as fair a name.
   Sound[116] them: it doth become[117] the mouth as well.   *145*
   Weigh them: it is as heavy. Conjure with 'em:[118]
   'Brutus' will start[119] a spirit as soon as 'Caesar'.

---

[108] *get the start of*: outstrip, outrun.

[109] *bear the palm*: be victorious (literally, carry off the palm of victory).

[110] *Shout. Flourish*: The shout corresponds with offer of the crown; the flourish, with Caesar's refusal of it.

[111] *bestride*: stand astride.

[112] *Colossus*: the Colossus of Rhodes, an enormous statue standing astride the harbor entrance, considered one of the seven wonders of the ancient world.

[113] *dishonourable graves*: i.e., as bondmen of Caesar.

[114] *stars*: fates (one's fate was believed to be partly determined by the position of the planets at one's birth).

[115] *sounded*: (1) spoken; (2) celebrated.

[116] *Sound*: speak.

[117] *doth become*: is befitting to.

[118] *Conjure with 'em*: The names of gods were believed to work as incantations in raising the dead.

[119] *start*: raise.

Now, in the names of all the gods at once,
Upon what meat[120] doth this our Caesar feed,
That he is grown so great? Age, thou art sham'd!   *150*
Rome, thou has lost the breed of noble bloods!
When went there by an age, since the great
    flood,[121]
But it was fam'd with[122] more than with one man?
When could they say, till now, that talk'd of
    Rome,
That her wide walls encompass'd but one man?   *155*
Now is it Rome indeed, and room[123] enough,
When there is in it but one only man.
O! you and I have heard our fathers say
There was a Brutus[124] once that would have
    brook'd[125]
Th' eternal devil to keep his state in Rome   *160*
As easily as a king.

Brutus. That you do love me, I am nothing
    jealous;[126]
What you would work[127] me to, I have some aim;[128]
How I have thought of this, and of these times,
I shall recount hereafter. For this present,   *165*
I would not, so with love I might entreat you,
Be any further mov'd. What you have said

[120] *meat*: food (generally).

[121] *great flood*: Ovid's *Metamorphosis*, like Genesis, told a story of a great flood in which Zeus punished the world for its wickedness, sparing only the virtuous Deucalion and his wife, Pyrrha.

[122] *fam'd with*: made famous because of.

[123] *Rome . . . room*: "Rome" was usually pronounced as a homonym of "room" during the Elizabethan period.

[124] *a Brutus*: i.e., Lucius Junius Brutus, one of the much-honored founders of the Roman Republic (509 B.C.), revered for the part he played in the overthrow of the tyrant Lucius Tarquinius Superbus (535–496 B.C.).

[125] *brook'd*: put up with, tolerated.

[126] *nothing jealous*: not at all suspicious.

[127] *work*: persuade.

[128] *aim*: (1) idea, notion; (2) intention.

I will consider; what you have to say
I will with patience hear; and find a time
Both meet[129] to hear and answer such high things.   *170*
Till then, my noble friend, chew[130] upon this:
Brutus had rather be a villager
Than to repute himself a son of Rome
Under these hard conditions as this time
Is like to lay upon us.   *175*

Cassius. I am glad that my weak words
 Have struck but thus much show of fire from
  Brutus.

Re-enter Caesar and his Train.[131]

Brutus. The games are done, and Caesar is
  returning.

Cassius. As they pass by, pluck Casca by the
  sleeve,
  And he will, after his sour fashion, tell you   *180*
  What hath proceeded worthy note to-day.

Brutus. I will do so. But, look you, Cassius,
  The angry spot doth glow on Caesar's brow,
  And all the rest look like a chidden[132] train;
  Calphurnia's cheek is pale, and Cicero   *185*
  Looks with such ferret[133] and such fiery eyes
  As we have seen him in the Capitol,
  Being cross'd in conference[134] by some senators.

Cassius. Casca will tell us what the matter is.

Caesar. Antonius!   *190*

---

[129] *meet*: fitting.
[130] *chew*: reflect, ruminate.
[131] *Train*: retainers and attendants.
[132] *chidden*: scolded.
[133] *ferret*: small, weasel-like creature.
[134] *conference*: debate.

Antony. Caesar?

Caesar. Let me have men about me that are fat;
    Sleek-headed men, and such as sleep o' nights.
    Yond[135] Cassius has a lean and hungry look;
    He thinks too much. Such men are dangerous.   *195*

Antony. Fear him not, Caesar, he's not
        dangerous;
    He is a noble Roman, and well given.[136]

Caesar. Would he were fatter! But I fear him not.
    Yet if my name were liable to fear,[137]
    I do not know the man I should avoid   *200*
    So soon as that spare Cassius. He reads much,
    He is a great observer, and he looks
    Quite through the deeds of men.[138] He loves no
        plays,
    As thou dost, Antony; he hears no music.[139]
    Seldom he smiles, and smiles in such a sort[140]   *205*
    As if he mock'd himself, and scorn'd his spirit
    That could be mov'd to smile at anything.
    Such men as he be never at heart's ease
    Whiles they behold a greater than themselves,
    And therefore are they very dangerous.   *210*
    I rather tell thee what is to be fear'd
    Than what I fear; for always I am Caesar.

---

[135] *Yond:* yonder.

[136] *well given:* well disposed.

[137] *if my name were liable to fear:* if fear could be associated with my name and reputation (i.e., with me).

[138] *through the deeds of men:* through men's deeds to see the motives underlying them.

[139] *no music:* The Greek philosopher Pythagoras (c. 570–c. 495 B.C.) argued that music symbolized metaphysical and physical harmony; thus: "The man that hath no music in himself, / Nor is not moved with concord of sweet sounds, / Is fit for treasons, stratagems, and spoils" (William Shakespeare, *The Merchant of Venice*, ed. Joseph Pearce, Ignatius Critical Editions [San Francisco: Ignatius Press, 2009], 5.1.83–85).

[140] *sort:* manner, way.

Come on my right hand, for this ear is deaf,
And tell me truly what thou think'st of him.

[*Sennet. Exeunt Caesar and his Train.*]

Casca. You pull'd me by the cloak. Would you
    speak with me?   *215*

Brutus. Ay, Casca; tell us what hath chanc'd
    to-day,
    That Caesar looks so sad?[141]

Casca. Why, you were with him, were you not?

Brutus. I should not then ask Casca what had chanc'd.

Casca. Why, there was a crown offer'd him; and   *220*
    being offer'd him, he put it by[142] with the back of
    his hand, thus; and then the people fell
    a-shouting.

Brutus. What was the second noise for?

Casca. Why, for that too.

Cassius. They shouted thrice; what was the last   *225*
    cry for?

Casca. Why, for that too.

Brutus. Was the crown offer'd him thrice?

Casca. Ay, marry,[143] was't, and he put it by thrice,
    every time gentler[144] than other; and at every
    putting by mine honest[145] neighbours[146] shouted.   *230*

---

[141] *sad*: grave, sorrowful.
[142] *put it by*: set it aside, rejected it.
[143] *marry*: indeed (colloquial expression, literally meaning "by the Virgin Mary").
[144] *gentler*: i.e., with greater reluctance.
[145] *honest*: when used of an inferior, usually meant in a patronizing manner.
[146] *neighbours*: (1) those standing near to him; (2) more generally, his fellow
men.

Cassius. Who offer'd him the crown?

Casca. Why, Antony.

Brutus. Tell us the manner of it, gentle Casca.

Casca. I can as well be hang'd as tell the manner
of it: it was mere foolery; I did not mark it. I saw
Mark Antony offer him a crown—yet 'twas not a
crown neither, 'twas one of these coronets[147]—
and, as I told you, he put it by once; but for all
that, to my thinking, he would fain[148] have had it.
Then he offered it to him again; then he put it
by again; but to my thinking, he was very loath
to lay his fingers off it. And then he offered it the
third time; he put it the third time by; and still
as[149] he refus'd it, the rabblement[150] hooted, and
clapp'd their chopt[151] hands, and threw up their
sweaty night-caps,[152] and uttered such a deal of
stinking breath because Caesar refus'd the
crown, that it had almost choked Caesar; for he
swounded[153] and fell down at it. And for mine own
part I durst not[154] laugh, for fear of opening my
lips and receiving the bad air.

Cassius. But soft,[155] I pray you. What, did Caesar   *250*
swound?

Casca. He fell down in the market-place, and
foam'd at mouth, and was speechless.

---

[147] *coronets*: small crowns.
[148] *fain*: gladly, happily.
[149] *still as*: every time.
[150] *rabblement*: rabble, lower-class mobs.
[151] *chopt*: chapped, rough from labor.
[152] *night-caps*: i.e., work caps (described derogatively here).
[153] *swounded*: swooned, fainted.
[154] *durst not*: would not have dared.
[155] *soft*: wait.

Brutus. 'Tis very like. He hath the falling
    sickness.[156]

Cassius. No, Caesar hath it not; but you, and I,
    And honest Casca, we have the falling sickness.[157] 255

Casca. I know not what you mean by that, but I
    am sure Caesar fell down. If the tag-rag people[158]
    did not clap him and hiss him, according as he
    pleas'd and displeas'd them, as they use[159] to do
    the players in the theatre, I am no true man.   260

Brutus. What said he when he came unto
    himself?

Casca. Marry, before he fell down, when he
    perceiv'd the common herd was glad he refus'd
    the crown, he pluckt me ope[160] his doublet,[161] and
    offer'd them his throat to cut. An I had been a
    man of any occupation,[162] if I would not have
    taken him at a word, I would I might go to hell
    among the rogues. And so he fell. When he
    came to himself again, he said, if he had done or
    said anything amiss, he desir'd their worships to
    think it was his infirmity. Three or four
    wenches, where I stood, cried 'Alas, good soul!'
    and forgave him with all their hearts. But there's
    no heed to be taken of them; if Caesar had
    stabb'd their mothers, they would have done no
    less.

Brutus. And after that, he came thus sad away?   275

[156] *falling sickness*: epilepsy (brain disorder prompting seizures).
[157] *falling sickness*: political collapse (meant figuratively here).
[158] *tag-rag people*: riffraff (wearing ragged clothing).
[159] *use*: are accustomed.
[160] *ope*: open.
[161] *doublet*: close-fitting sleeveless jacket worn in Shakespeare's time (not in the Roman Republic).
[162] *man of any occupation*: (1) man of the working class; (2) decisive man of action.

Casca. Ay.

Cassius. Did Cicero say anything?

Casca. Ay, he spoke Greek.[163]

Cassius. To what effect?

Casca. Nay, an[164] I tell you that, I'll ne'er look you i'   280
     th' face again. But those that understood him
     smil'd at one another, and shook their heads;
     but for mine own part, it was Greek to me. I
     could tell you more news too: Marullus and
     Flavius, for pulling scarfs[165] off Caesar's images,
     are put to silence.[166] Fare you well. There was   285
     more foolery yet, if I could remember it.

Cassius. Will you sup with me to-night, Casca?

Casca. No, I am promis'd forth.[167]

Cassius. Will you dine with me to-morrow?

Casca. Ay, if I be alive, and your mind hold,[168] and   290
     your dinner worth the eating.

Cassius. Good; I will expect you.

Casca. Do so. Farewell, both.   [*Exit.*]

Brutus. What a blunt[169] fellow is this grown to be!
     He was quick mettle[170] when he went to school.   295

Cassius. So is he now, in execution
     Of any bold or noble enterprise,

---

[163] *Greek*: Only the upper classes spoke Greek.

[164] *an*: if.

[165] *scarfs*: (1) scrolls; (2) sashes.

[166] *put to silence*: deprived of their tribuneships and possibly exiled (perhaps executed, but not a very likely eventuality).

[167] *am promis'd forth*: have a previous engagement or commitment.

[168] *hold*: remain unchanged, be resolute.

[169] *blunt*: (1) abrupt, to the point; (2) dull, stupid.

[170] *quick mettle*: quick spirit or playful disposition.

However he puts on this tardy form.[171]
This rudeness is a sauce to his good wit,[172]
Which gives men stomach[173] to disgest[174] his words   300
With better appetite.

Brutus. And so it is. For this time I will leave
          you.
     To-morrow, if you please to speak with me,
     I will come home to you; or, if you will,
     Come home to me, and I will wait for you.   305

Cassius. I will do so. Till then, think of the
          world.[175]   [*Exit Brutus.*]
     Well, Brutus, thou art noble; yet, I see,
     Thy honourable mettle[176] may be wrought
     From that it is dispos'd.[177] Therefore it is meet[178]
     That noble minds keep ever with their likes;   310
     For who so firm that cannot be seduc'd?
     Caesar doth bear me hard;[179] but he loves Brutus.
     If I were Brutus now and he were Cassius,
     He should not humour[180] me. I will this night,
     In several hands,[181] in at his windows throw,   315
     As if they came from several citizens,
     Writings, all tending to[182] the great opinion
     That Rome holds of his name; wherein
          obscurely[183]

[171] *tardy form*: rough or sluggish manner.
[172] *wit*: intelligence.
[173] *stomach*: capacity, appetite.
[174] *disgest*: digest.
[175] *world*: i.e., the present world situation.
[176] *mettle*: temperament (a metallurgical metaphor).
[177] *wrought / From that it is dispos'd*: formed into something other than its natural shape.
[178] *meet*: fitting.
[179] *doth bear me hard*: holds a grudge against me.
[180] *humour*: persuade, cajole.
[181] *several hands*: different handwritings.
[182] *tending to*: expressing.
[183] *obscurely*: vaguely, cryptically.

Caesar's ambition shall be glanced[184] at.
And, after this, let Caesar seat him sure;[185]   *320*
For we will shake him, or worse days endure.

[*Exit.*]

Scene 3. *Rome. A street.*

*Thunder and lightning. Enter, from opposite sides,
Casca, with his sword drawn, and Cicero.*

Cicero. Good even,[186] Casca. Brought you Caesar
   home?
   Why are you breathless? and why stare you so?

Casca. Are not you mov'd, when all the sway of
      earth[187]
   Shakes like a thing unfirm?[188] O Cicero,
   I have seen tempests when the scolding winds   5
   Have riv'd[189] the knotty oaks, and I have seen
   Th' ambitious ocean swell, and rage, and foam,
   To be exalted with[190] the threat'ning clouds;
   But never till to-night, never till now,
   Did I go through a tempest dropping fire.   10
   Either there is a civil strife in heaven,
   Or else the world, too saucy with the gods,
   Incenses them to send destruction.

Cicero. Why, saw you any thing more[191]
   wonderful?

184 *glanced*: hinted.
185 *seat him sure*: settle himself securely.
186 *even*: evening.
187 *all the sway of earth*: the whole world order, everything.
188 *unfirm*: infirm.
189 *riv'd*: split.
190 *exalted with*: raised up to.
191 *more*: else.

Casca. A common slave—you know him well by
  sight—   15
Held up his left hand, which did flame and burn
Like twenty torches join'd; and yet his hand,
Not sensible of[192] fire, remain'd unscorch'd.
Besides—I ha' not since put up[193] my sword—
Against[194] the Capitol I met a lion,   20
Who glaz'd[195] upon me, and went surly by
Without annoying[196] me; and there were drawn
Upon a heap[197] a hundred ghastly[198] women,
Transformed with their fear, who swore they
  saw
Men, all in fire, walk up and down the streets.   25
And yesterday the bird of night[199] did sit,
Even at noon-day, upon the market-place,
Hooting and shrieking. When these prodigies[200]
Do so conjointly meet,[201] let not men say
'These are their reasons—they are natural',   30
For I believe they are portentous things
Unto the climate[202] that they point upon.[203]

Cicero. Indeed, it is a strange-disposed[204] time;
  But men may construe things after their fashion,[205]

[192] *sensible of*: sensitive to.
[193] *put up*: sheathed.
[194] *Against*: opposite to, nearby.
[195] *glaz'd*: stared fixedly (glassily).
[196] *annoying*: harming, bothering.
[197] *drawn / Upon a heap*: crowded together.
[198] *ghastly*: white-faced, like ghosts.
[199] *bird of night*: owl or raven, birds of ill omen.
[200] *prodigies*: omens, unnatural events.
[201] *conjointly meet*: join together.
[202] *climate*: region or place.
[203] *they are portentous things . . . they point upon*: It was commonly believed during antiquity and during the Elizabethan period that the stars could have an influence (probably malign) on men.
[204] *strange-disposed*: inclined toward the abnormal.
[205] *after their fashion*: however they like, in their own way.

Clean from the purpose[206] of the things
    themselves.   35
Comes Caesar to the Capitol to-morrow?

Casca. He doth; for he did bid Antonius
    Send word to you he would be there to-morrow.

Cicero. Good night, then, Casca; this disturbed
    sky
Is not to walk in.   40

Casca.   Farewell, Cicero.   [*Exit Cicero.*]

Enter Cassius.

Cassius. Who's there?

Casca.   A Roman.

Cassius.   Casca, by your voice.

Casca. Your ear is good. Cassius, what night is
    this!

Cassius. A very pleasing night to honest men.

Casca. Who ever knew the heavens menace so?

Cassius. Those that have known the earth so full
    of faults.   45
    For my part, I have walk'd about the streets,
    Submitting me unto the perilous night,
    And, thus unbraced,[207] Casca, as you see,
    Have bar'd my bosom to the thunder-stone;[208]
    And when the cross[209] blue lighting seem'd to
        open   50
    The breast of heaven, I did present myself
    Even in the aim and very flash of it.

---

[206] *Clean from the purpose*: contrary to the true bearing of the case.
[207] *unbraced*: unfastened, unbuttoned.
[208] *thunder-stone*: thunderbolt (in classical mythology, wielded by the gods).
[209] *cross*: forked.

Casca. But wherefore did you so much tempt the
    heavens?
  It is the part[210] of men to fear and tremble
  When the most mighty gods by tokens[211] send   55
  Such dreadful heralds to astonish[212] us.

Cassius. You are dull, Casca, and those sparks of
    life
  That should be in a Roman you do want,[213]
  Or else you use not. You look pale, and gaze,
  And put on[214] fear, and cast yourself in wonder,[215]   60
  To see the strange impatience of the heavens;
  But if you would consider the true cause—
  Why all these fires, why all these gliding ghosts,
  Why birds and beasts, from quality and kind;[216]
  Why old men, fools, and children calculate;[217]   65
  Why all these things change from their
    ordinance,[218]
  Their natures and preformed[219] faculties,
  To monstrous[220] quality—why, you shall find
  That heaven hath infus'd them with these
    spirits,[221]
  To make them instruments of fear and warning   70
  Unto some monstrous state.[222]
  Now could I, Casca, name to thee a man

[210] *part*: role.

[211] *tokens*: signs.

[212] *astonish*: stun, startle.

[213] *want*: lack.

[214] *put on*: show, display.

[215] *cast yourself in wonder*: are amazed.

[216] *from quality and kind*: against their natures.

[217] *old men, fools, and children calculate*: "Calculate" means to foretell or prophesy; cf. an old proverb: "Fools and children often prophesy."

[218] *ordinance*: naturally ordained order.

[219] *preformed*: inherent, congenital.

[220] *monstrous*: unnatural.

[221] *spirits*: supernatural powers.

[222] *Unto some monstrous state*: gesturing toward some fearful, abnormal condition.

Most like this dreadful night
That thunders, lightens, opens graves, and roars
As doth the lion in the Capitol; 75
A man no mightier than thyself or me
In personal action, yet prodigious[223] grown,
And fearful,[224] as these strange eruptions[225] are.

Casca. 'Tis Caesar that you mean, is it not,
Cassius?

Cassius. Let it be who it is; for Romans now 80
Have thews[226] and limbs like to their ancestors.
But woe the while![227] our fathers' minds are dead,
And we are govern'd with our mothers' spirits;
Our yoke and sufferance[228] show us womanish.

Casca. Indeed they say the senators to-morrow 85
Mean to establish Caesar as a king;
And he shall wear his crown by sea and land,
In every place save here in Italy.

Cassius. I know where I will wear this dagger
then;[229]
Cassius from bondage will deliver Cassius. 90
Therein,[230] ye gods, you make the weak most
strong;
Therein, ye gods, you tyrants do defeat.
Nor stony tower, nor walls of beaten brass,
Nor airless dungeon, nor strong links of iron,
Can be retentive to[231] the strength of spirit; 95

[223] *prodigious*: unnatural, extraordinary, ominous.
[224] *fearful*: fear inducing.
[225] *eruptions*: upheavals in nature.
[226] *thews*: muscles and tendons.
[227] *woe the while*: alas for these times.
[228] *yoke and sufferance*: servitude and meek submission to it.
[229] *where I will wear this dagger then*: i.e., in his own chest.
[230] *Therein*: i.e., in suicide.
[231] *be retentive to*: hold in, retain.

But life, being weary of these worldly bars,
Never lacks power to dismiss itself.
If I know this, know all the world besides,
That part of tyranny that I do bear,
I can shake off at pleasure.   [*Thunder still.*]

Casca.   So can I;   100
So every bondman[232] in his own hand bears
The power to cancel his captivity.

Cassius. And why should Caesar be a tyrant,
    then?
Poor man! I know he would not be a wolf
But that he sees the Romans are but sheep;[233]   105
He were no lion, were not Romans hinds.[234]
Those that with haste will make a mighty fire
Begin it with weak straws. What trash is Rome,
What rubbish, and what offal,[235] when it serves
For the base[236] matter[237] to illuminate   110
So vile a thing as Caesar! But, O grief,
Where hast thou led me? I perhaps speak this
Before a willing bondman; then I know
My answer must be made.[238] But I am arm'd,
And dangers are to me indifferent.[239]   115

Casca. You speak to Casca, and to such a man
    That is no fleering[240] tell-tale. Hold,[241] my hand.[242]

[232] *bondman*: slave.
[233] *he would not be a wolf . . . Romans are but sheep*: Cf. the proverb: "He that makes himself a sheep shall be eaten by the wolf."
[234] *hinds*: (1) peasants, menials; (2) female deer.
[235] *offal*: refuse, trash.
[236] *base*: debased, morally low.
[237] *matter*: (1) substance, material; (2) fuel.
[238] *My answer must be made*: I shall have to accept the consequences of my words.
[239] *indifferent*: of no importance.
[240] *fleering*: mocking, jeering. Some versions read "fleeting".
[241] *Hold*: Enough (of this).
[242] *my hand*: Brutus is proffering his hand to be shaken.

Be factious[243] for redress of all these griefs,[244]
And I will set this foot of mine as far
As who goes farthest.

Cassius.   There's a bargain made.   *120*
Now know you, Casca, I have mov'd already
Some certain of the noblest-minded Romans
To undergo[245] with me an enterprise
Of honourable-dangerous consequence;
And I do know by this[246] they stay for me   *125*
In Pompey's porch;[247] for now, this fearful night,
There is no stir or walking in the streets,
And the complexion of the element[248]
In favour's like[249] the work we have in hand,
Most bloody, fiery, and most terrible.   *130*

Enter Cinna.

Casca. Stand close[250] awhile, for here comes one in
    haste.

Cassius. 'Tis Cinna, I do know him by his gait;
    He is a friend. Cinna, where haste you so?

Cinna. To find out you. Who's that? Metellus
    Cimber?

Cassius. No, it is Casca, one incorporate[251]   *135*
    To our attempts. Am I not stay'd for,[252] Cinna?

[243] *Be factious*: form a political faction.
[244] *griefs*: grievances.
[245] *undergo*: undertake.
[246] *by this*: by now.
[247] *Pompey's porch*: the portico of Pompey's theater (where a statue of Pompey was prominently displayed). (According to Plutarch, Caesar was assassinated at the theater, not at the Capitol.)
[248] *complexion of the element*: appearance or disposition of the sky.
[249] *In favor's like*: appears like, seems in appearance like.
[250] *close*: (1) hidden; (2) still or silent.
[251] *incorporate/To*: an integral part of, associated with.
[252] *stay'd for*: awaited.

Cinna. I am glad on't.[253] What a fearful night is this!
　There's two or three of us have seen strange
　　sights.

Cassius. Am I not stay'd for? Tell me.

Cinna. Yes, you are. O Cassius, if you could   140
　But win the noble Brutus to our party—

Cassius. Be you content. Good Cinna, take this
　　paper,
　And look you lay it in the praetor's chair,[254]
　Where Brutus may but find it;[255] and throw this
　In at his window; set this up with wax[256]   145
　Upon old Brutus'[257] statue. All this done,
　Repair[258] to Pompey's porch, where you shall find
　　us.
　Is Decius Brutus[259] and Trebonius there?

Cinna. All but Metellus Cimber, and he's gone
　To seek you at your house. Well, I will hie,[260]   150
　And so bestow these papers as you bade me.

Cassius. That done, repair to Pompey's theatre.

　　　　　　　　　　　　　　　　[*Exit Cinna.*]

　Come, Casca, you and I will yet ere day
　See Brutus at his house. Three parts of him

---

[253] *on't*: on it, for it (i.e., for their growing conspiracy).

[254] *praetor's chair*: official chair of the chief magistrate (i.e., Brutus).

[255] *may but find it*: (1) must certainly find it; (2) will be the only one to find it.

[256] *set this up with wax*: Proclamations or epitaphs were frequently attached to walls or monuments by use of wax.

[257] *old Brutus' statue*: i.e., the statue of the founder Lucius Junius Brutus.

[258] *Repair*: go.

[259] *Decius Brutus*: Decimus Brutus (c. 81–42 B.C.), kinsman of and fellow conspirator with Marcus Brutus (the misspelling of his name is taken from the translation of Plutarch most likely read by Shakespeare).

[260] *hie*: hurry.

Is ours already, and the man entire   *155*
Upon the next encounter yields him ours.

Casca. O, he sits high in all the people's hearts;
And that which would appear offence in us
His countenance,[261] like richest alchemy,[262]
Will change to virtue[263] and to worthiness.[264]   *160*

Cassius. Him and his worth and our great need
   of him
You have right well conceited.[265] Let us go,
For it is after midnight; and ere day
We will awake him and be sure of him.

[*Exeunt.*]

[261] *countenance*: support.
[262] *alchemy*: chemical study (believed magical) for converting base metals into gold or other noble metals.
[263] *virtue*: the highest moral value or quality.
[264] *worthiness*: nobility.
[265] *conceited*: (1) understood; (2) expressed in elaborate or poetic terms.

ACT 2

Scene 1. *Rome.*

Enter Brutus in his orchard.[1]

Brutus. What, Lucius, ho!
  I cannot by the progress of the stars
  Give guess how near to day. Lucius, I say!
  I would it were my fault to sleep so soundly.
  When, Lucius, when? Awake, I say! What,
    Lucius!   5

Enter Lucius.

Lucius. Call'd you, my lord?

Brutus. Get me a taper[2] in my study, Lucius;
  When it is lighted, come and call me here.

Lucius. I will, my lord.   [*Exit.*]

Brutus. It must be by his death; and for my part,   10
  I know no personal cause to spurn at[3] him,
  But for the general:[4] he would be crown'd.
  How that might change his nature, there's the
    question.
  It is the bright day that brings forth the adder,
  And that craves[5] wary walking. Crown him
    —that![6]   15
  And then, I grant, we put a sting in him
  That at his will he may do danger[7] with.
  Th' abuse of greatness is, when it disjoins

[1] *orchard*: garden.
[2] *taper*: candle.
[3] *spurn at*: kick out against (in rebellion).
[4] *general*: common good.
[5] *craves*: demands, dearly requires.
[6] *Crown him—that*: (1) crown him—king; (2) crown him—crown *that man.*
[7] *danger*: harm.

34

Remorse[8] from power; and to speak truth of
    Caesar,
I have not known when his affections sway'd[9]   20
More than his reason. But 'tis a common proof[10]
That lowliness[11] is young ambition's ladder,
Whereto the climber-upward turns his face;
But when he once attains the upmost round,[12]
He then unto the ladder turns his back,   25
Looks in the clouds, scorning the base degrees[13]
By which he did ascend. So Caesar may.
Then, lest he may, prevent. And since the
    quarrel
Will bear no colour[14] for the thing he is,
Fashion it thus[15]—that what he is, augmented,   30
Would run to these and these extremities;[16]
And therefore think him as a serpent's egg,
Which, hatch'd, would as his kind[17] grow
    mischievous,[18]
And kill him in the shell.[19]

Re-enter Lucius.

[8] *Remorse:* (1) mercy; (2) conscience.

[9] *affections sway'd:* emotions or passions ruled his actions.

[10] *common proof:* fact proved by general experience.

[11] *lowliness:* humility.

[12] *round:* rung (i.e., of the ladder).

[13] *base degrees:* (1) lower steps of the ladder; (2) the common people or, indeed, anyone lower in rank.

[14] *the quarrel / Will bear no colour:* the cause or subject for complaint will have no plausible reason to color it.

[15] *Fashion it thus:* present it in this manner.

[16] *these and these extremities:* such and such conclusions (the extremes of tyranny).

[17] *as his kind:* according to its (i.e., the serpent's) nature.

[18] *mischievous:* dangerous, vicious.

[19] *kill him in the shell:* It was proverbially recommended that a creature such as the cockatrice (a mythical creature like a basilisk, fabled to kill by its glance) be killed while still in its shell.

Lucius. The taper burneth in your closet,[20] sir.   35
   Searching the window for a flint, I found
   This paper, thus seal'd up; and I am sure
   It did not lie there when I went to bed.

                              [*Giving him a letter.*]

Brutus. Get you to bed again, it is not day.
   Is not to-morrow, boy, the ides of March?   40

Lucius. I know not, sir.

Brutus. Look in the calender, and bring me
      word.

Lucius. I will, sir.   [*Exit.*]

Brutus. The exhalations,[21] whizzing in the air,
   Give so much light that I may read by them.   45

                    [*Opens the letter and reads.*]

   'Brutus, thou sleep'st. Awake, and see thyself.
   Shall Rome, etc. Speak, strike, redress!
   Brutus, thou sleep'st; awake.'
   Such instigations have been often dropp'd
   Where I have took them up.   50
   'Shall Rome, &c.'[22] Thus must I piece it out:[23]
   Shall Rome stand under one man's awe?[24] What,
      Rome?
   My ancestors did from the streets of Rome
   The Tarquin drive, when he was call'd a king.
   'Speak, strike, redress!' Am I entreated   55
   To speak and strike? O Rome, I make thee
      promise,

[20] *closet*: study, private room.
[21] *exhalations*: meteors.
[22] *&c*: et cetera.
[23] *piece it out*: work it out, develop this point.
[24] *under one man's awe*: in awe of or subject to one man's power.

If the redress will follow, thou receivest
Thy full petition at the hand of[25] Brutus!

Re-enter Lucius.

Lucius. Sir, March is wasted fifteen days.[26]

                       [*Knocking within.*]

Brutus. 'Tis good. Go to the gate; somebody
   knocks.   [*Exit Lucius.*] 60
Since Cassius first did whet[27] me against Caesar,
   I have not slept.
Between the acting of a dreadful thing
And the first motion,[28] all the interim is
Like a phantasma[29] or a hideous dream.   65
The Genius[30] and the mortal instruments[31]
Are then in council; and the state of man,[32]
Like to a little kingdom, suffers then
The nature of[33] an insurrection.

Re-enter Lucius.

Lucius. Sir, 'tis your brother[34] Cassius at the door 70
Who doth desire to see you.

Brutus.   Is he alone?

Lucius. No, sir, there are moe[35] with him.

Brutus.   Do you know them?

[25] *Thy full petition at the hand of*: all you request from.
[26] *March is wasted fifteen days*: I.e., it is March 15.
[27] *whet*: incite.
[28] *motion*: impulse.
[29] *phantasma*: hallucination.
[30] *Genius*: guardian spirit, reasoning spirit.
[31] *mortal instruments*: emotions and physical abilities.
[32] *state of man*: (1) the human condition; (2) the realm in which men live.
[33] *The nature of*: a kind of.
[34] *brother*: brother-in-law (Cassius was married to a sister of Brutus).
[35] *moe*: more.

Lucius. No, sir; their hats are pluck'd about their
   ears
  And half their faces buried in their cloaks,
  That by no means I may discover[36] them   75
  By any mark of favour.[37]

Brutus.   Let 'em enter.

                          [*Exit Lucius.*]

  They are the faction. O conspiracy,
  Sham'st thou to show thy dang'rous brow by
   night,
  When evils[38] are most free? O, then by day
  Where wilt thou find a cavern dark enough   80
  To mask thy monstrous visage? Seek none,
   conspiracy;
  Hide it in smiles and affability!
  For if thou path,[39] thy native semblance[40] on,
  Not Erebus[41] itself were dim enough
  To hide thee from prevention.[42]   85

Enter the conspirators, Cassius, Casca, Decius, Cinna,
Metellus Cimber, and Trebonius.

Cassius. I think we are too bold[43] upon your rest.
  Good morrow, Brutus. Do we trouble you?

Brutus. I have been up this hour, awake all night.
  Know I these men that come along with you?

---

[36] *discover:* recognize.

[37] *mark of favour:* feature of appearance.

[38] *evils:* evil thoughts or things.

[39] *path:* pursue this path.

[40] *native semblance:* true, natural appearance.

[41] *Erebus:* in classical mythology, the dark passage between the earth and Hades, the underworld.

[42] *prevention:* being hindered.

[43] *are too bold:* interrupt presumptuously.

Cassius. Yes, every man of them; and no man here   90
  But honours you; and every one doth wish
  You had but that opinion of yourself
  Which every noble Roman bears of you.
  This is Trebonius.

Brutus.   He is welcome hither.

Cassius. This, Decius Brutus.

Brutus.   He is welcome too.   95

Cassius. This, Casca; this, Cinna;
  And this, Metellus Cimber.

Brutus.   They are all welcome.
  What watchful cares[44] do interpose themselves
  Betwixt your eyes and night?

Cassius. Shall I entreat a word?   [*They whisper.*] 100

Decius. Here lies the east. Doth not the day break here?

Casca. No.

Cinna. O, pardon, sir, it doth; and yon grey lines
  That fret[45] the clouds are messengers of day.

Casca. You shall confess that you are both deceiv'd.[46]   105
  Here, as I point my sword, the sun arises;
  Which is a great way growing on[47] the south,
  Weighing[48] the youthful season of the year.
  Some two months hence up higher toward the north   110

---

[44] *watchful cares*: problems that have kept them awake.
[45] *fret*: interlace.
[46] *deceiv'd*: mistaken (i.e., regarding the sky).
[47] *growing on*: headed toward.
[48] *Weighing*: considering.

He first presents his fire; and the high[49] east
Stands as the Capitol, directly here.

Brutus. Give me your hands all over,[50] one by one.

Cassius. And let us swear our resolution.

Brutus. No, not an oath. If not the face of men,[51]
   The sufferance[52] of our souls, the time's abuse,[53]   *115*
   If these be motives weak, break off betimes,[54]
   And every man hence to his idle[55] bed.
   So let high-sighted tyranny[56] range[57] on,
   Till each man drop by lottery.[58] But if these,
   As I am sure they do, bear fire enough   *120*
   To kindle cowards, and to steel with valour
   The melting spirits of women, then,
      countrymen,
   What need we any spur but our own cause
   To prick[59] us to redress? What other bond
   Than secret Romans[60] that have spoke the word   *125*
   And will not palter?[61] And what other oath
   Than honesty[62] to honesty engag'd[63]

---

[49] *high*: due.

[50] *all over*: all of you, everyone.

[51] *the face of men*: their countenances (which should be a sign of their sincerity).

[52] *sufferance*: endurance.

[53] *time's abuse*: the corruption of the present age (i.e., Caesar's unconstitutional rise).

[54] *betimes*: early (i.e., now).

[55] *idle*: inactive.

[56] *high-sighted tyranny*: (1) ambitious tyranny setting its sights high; (2) tyranny that sits high like a bird of prey that can swoop down at any moment as it so wills.

[57] *range*: prowl or fly in search of prey.

[58] *lottery*: chance (i.e., at the whim of a tyrant).

[59] *prick*: urge, provoke.

[60] *secret Romans*: Romans capable of preserving secrecy (because of their integrity).

[61] *palter*: equivocate.

[62] *honesty*: personal honor.

[63] *engag'd*: pledged, sworn.

That this shall be or we will fall for it?
Swear priests and cowards and men cautelous,[64]
Old feeble carrions[65] and such suffering souls   *130*
That welcome wrongs; unto bad causes swear
Such creatures as men doubt; but do not stain
The even[66] virtue of our enterprise,
Nor th' insuppressive mettle[67] of our spirits,
To think that or our cause or[68] our performance   *135*
Did need an oath; when every drop of blood
That every Roman bears, and nobly bears,
Is guilty of a several bastardy,[69]
If he do break the smallest particle
Of any promise that hath pass'd from him.   *140*

Cassius. But what of Cicero? Shall we sound
    him?
I think he will stand very strong with us.

Casca. Let us not leave him out.

Cinna.   No, by no means.

Metellus. O, let us have him; for his silver hairs
Will purchase us a good opinion,[70]   *145*
And buy men's voices to commend our deeds.
It shall be said his judgment rul'd our hands;
Our youths and wildness shall no whit[71] appear,
But all be buried in his gravity.[72]

Brutus. O, name him not! Let us not break with[73]
    him;   *150*

---

[64] *cautelous*: (1) cautious; (2) deceitful.
[65] *carrions*: rotting wretches (alive or dead).
[66] *even*: unblemished.
[67] *insuppressive mettle*: indomitable quality or spirit.
[68] *or . . . or* : either.
[69] *guilty of a several bastardy*: guilty of acts that are not truly Roman.
[70] *opinion*: reputation.
[71] *no whit*: not at all.
[72] *gravity*: sobriety, seriousness.
[73] *break with*: present, outline our plan to.

For he will never follow any thing
That other men begin.

Cassius.   Then leave him out.

Casca. Indeed he is not fit.

Decius. Shall no man else be touch'd but only
    Caesar?

Cassius. Decius, well urg'd.[74] I think it is not meet   *155*
Mark Antony, so well belov'd of Caesar,
Should outlive Caesar. We shall find of[75] him
A shrewd contriver;[76] and you know his means,
If he improve[77] them, may well stretch so far
As to annoy[78] us all; which to prevent,   *160*
Let Antony and Caesar fall together.

Brutus. Our course will seem too bloody, Caius
    Cassius,
To cut the head off and then hack the limbs—
Like wrath in death and envy[79] afterwards;
For Antony is but a limb[80] of Caesar.   *165*
Let's be sacrificers, but not butchers, Caius.
We all stand up against the spirit of Caesar,[81]
And in the spirit of men there is no blood.
O that we then could come by[82] Caesar's spirit,
And not dismember Caesar! But, alas,   *170*
Caesar must bleed for it! And, gentle friends,
Let's kill him boldly, but not wrathfully;
Let's carve him as a dish fit for the gods,

---

[74] *urg'd*: argued.

[75] *of*: in.

[76] *shrewd contriver*: cunning schemer (against the conspirators).

[77] *improve*: use to the utmost.

[78] *annoy*: harm.

[79] *envy*: maliciousness (i.e., as if they were killing Caesar out of hatred and envy).

[80] *limb*: dependent.

[81] *spirit of Caesar*: i.e., the tyranny Caesar represents.

[82] *come by*: get a hold of.

Not hew him as a carcase fit for hounds;
And let our hearts, as subtle masters do,   175
Stir up their servants[83] to an act of rage,
And after seem to chide 'em. This shall make
Our purpose necessary, and not envious;[84]
Which so appearing to the common eyes,
We shall be call'd purgers,[85] not murderers.   180
And for Mark Antony, think not of him;
For he can do no more than Caesar's arm
When Caesar's head is off.

Cassius.   Yet I fear him;
For in the engrafted[86] love he bears to Caesar—

Brutus. Alas, good Cassius, do not think of him!   185
If he love Caesar, all that he can do
Is to himself take thought[87] and die for Caesar;
And that were much he should,[88] for he is given
To sports, to wildness, and much company.

Trebonius. There is no fear[89] in him. Let him not
    die;   190
For he will live, and laugh at this hereafter.

                    [Clock strikes.[90]]

Brutus. Peace! Count the clock.

Cassius.   The clock hath stricken three.

Trebonius. 'Tis time to part.

Cassius.   But it is doubtful yet
Whether Caesar will come forth to-day or no;

[83] *servants*: i.e., the passions.
[84] *envious*: spiteful.
[85] *purgers*: healers (through purging, a common medicinal procedure).
[86] *engrafted*: deeply implanted.
[87] *take thought*: brood, turn melancholic.
[88] *were much he should*: would be more than should be expected of him.
[89] *no fear*: nothing to fear.
[90] *Clock strikes*: The striking clock was a medieval invention.

For he is superstitious grown of late, 195
Quite from the main[91] opinion he held once
Of fantasy, of dreams, and ceremonies.[92]
It may be these apparent prodigies,[93]
The unaccustom'd terror of this night,
And the persuasion of his augurers,[94] 200
May hold him from the Capitol to-day.

Decius. Never fear that. If he be so resolv'd,
I can o'ersway[95] him; for he loves to hear
That unicorns may be betray'd with trees,[96]
And bears with glasses,[97] elephants with holes,[98] 205
Lions with toils,[99] and men with flatterers;
But when I tell him he hates flatterers,
He says he does, being then most flattered.
Let me work;
For I can give his humour[100] the true bent,[101] 210
And I will bring him to the Capitol.

Cassius. Nay, we will all of us be there to fetch
him.

Brutus. By the eighth hour. Is that the
uttermost?[102]

Cinna. Be that the uttermost, and fail not then.

---

[91] *main*: strong.

[92] *ceremonies*: rites (to divulge omens).

[93] *apparent prodigies*: clear signs of pending disaster.

[94] *augurers*: priests who interpret omens.

[95] *o'ersway*: persuade.

[96] *unicorns may be betray'd with trees*: A tactic for capturing the legendary beast (the unicorn) was to tempt it to charge, then duck behind a tree, so that the horn would stick into the trunk, rendering the beast helpless.

[97] *glasses*: mirrors (bewildering the bear).

[98] *holes*: pitfalls (to trap animals).

[99] *toils*: snares (to trap animals).

[100] *humour*: temperament.

[101] *true bent*: the right direction.

[102] *uttermost*: latest.

Metellus. Caius Ligarius doth bear Caesar hard,[103]   215
    Who rated[104] him for speaking well of Pompey.
    I wonder none of you have thought of him.

Brutus. Now, good Metellus, go along by him.[105]
    He loves me well, and I have given him reasons;
    Send him but hither, and I'll fashion[106] him.   220

Cassius. The morning comes upon's. We'll leave
    you, Brutus.
    And, friends, disperse yourselves; but all
    remember
    What you have said, and show yourselves true
    Romans.

Brutus. Good gentlemen, look fresh and merrily;
    Let not our looks put on[107] our purposes,   225
    But bear it[108] as our Roman actors do,[109]
    With untir'd spirits and formal constancy.[110]
    And so good morrow to you every one.

                         [Exeunt all but Brutus.]

Boy! Lucius! Fast asleep? It is no matter;
Enjoy the honey-heavy dew[111] of slumber.   230
Thou hast no figures nor no fantasies[112]
Which busy care draws in the brains of men;
Therefore thou sleep'st so sound.

Enter Portia.

---

[103] *doth bear Caesar hard:* bears a grudge against Caesar.

[104] *rated:* berated.

[105] *by him:* to where he is (i.e., his house).

[106] *fashion:* work upon, shape (persuading him to their designs).

[107] *put on:* reveal.

[108] *it:* i.e., their parts.

[109] *as our Roman actors do:* In fact, Roman actors wore masks; Elizabethans did not (and are described here).

[110] *formal constancy:* steadfast observance of proper external appearances.

[111] *dew:* refreshment.

[112] *figures . . . fantasies:* figments of his imagination.

Portia. Brutus, my lord!

Brutus. Portia, what mean you? Wherefore rise
    you now?
  It is not for your health thus to commit   235
  Your weak condition to the raw cold morning.

Portia. Nor for yours neither. Y'have ungently,[113]
    Brutus,
  Stole from my bed; and yesternight at supper
  You suddenly arose and walk'd about,
  Musing and sighing, with your arms across;[114]   240
  And when I ask'd you what the matter was,
  You star'd upon me with ungentle looks.
  I urg'd you further; then you scratch'd your
    head
  And too impatiently stamp'd with your foot.
  Yet[115] I insisted; yet you answer'd not,   245
  But with an angry wafture[116] of your hand
  Gave sign for me to leave you. So I did,
  Fearing to strengthen that impatience
  Which seem'd too much enkindled; and withal[117]
  Hoping it was but an effect of humour,[118]   250
  Which sometimes hath his[119] hour with every
    man.
  It will not let you eat, nor talk, nor sleep;
  And, could it work so much upon your shape
  As it hath much prevail'd on your condition,[120]
  I should not know you[121] Brutus. Dear my lord,   255
  Make me acquainted with your cause of grief.

[113] *ungently*: discourteously.
[114] *across*: i.e., folded (showing that he was stuck in thought).
[115] *Yet*: still.
[116] *wafture*: wave.
[117] *withal*: with, thereby.
[118] *effect of humour*: result from a passing mood.
[119] *his*: its.
[120] *condition*: state of mind, disposition.
[121] *know you*: recognize you as.

Brutus. I am not well in health, and that is all.

Portia. Brutus is wise, and, were he not in health,
   He would embrace the means to come by it.

Brutus. Why, so I do. Good Portia, go to bed.   260

Portia. Is Brutus sick, and is it physical[122]
   To walk unbraced[123] and suck up the humours[124]
   Of the dank morning? What, is Brutus sick,
   And will he steal out of his wholesome bed,
   To dare the vile contagion of the night,[125]   265
   And tempt the rheumy and unpurged[126] air
   To add unto his sickness? No, my Brutus;
   You have some sick offence[127] within your mind,
   Which by the right and virtue of my place[128]
   I ought to know of; and upon my knees   270
   I charm[129] you, by my once-commended beauty,
   By all your vows of love, and that great vow
   Which did incorporate and make us one,[130]
   That you unfold to me, your self, your half,
   Why you are heavy[131]—and what men to-night   275
   Have had resort to you; for here have been
   Some six or seven, who did hide their faces
   Even from darkness.

Brutus.   Kneel not, gentle Portia.

---

[122] *physical*: healthy.

[123] *unbraced*: with clothes unfastened.

[124] *humours*: dampness (affecting the humors of the human body).

[125] *vile contagion of the night*: The night air was considered to have a deeply harmful and even poisonous effect on men.

[126] *rheumy and unpurged*: damp and unpurified.

[127] *sick offense*: unwholesome disturbance.

[128] *place*: position (as a wife).

[129] *charm*: entreat.

[130] *incorporate and make us one*: make us one flesh through marriage (cf. Matthew 19:5).

[131] *heavy*: heavy hearted.

Portia. I should not need, if you were gentle
    Brutus.
  Within the bond of marriage, tell me, Brutus,   *280*
  Is it excepted[132] I should know no secrets
  That appertain to you? Am I your self
  But, as it were, in sort or limitation?[133]
  To keep[134] with you at meals, comfort[135] your bed,
  And talk to you sometimes? Dwell I but in the
    suburbs[136]   *285*
  Of your good pleasure? If it be no more,
  Portia is Brutus' harlot, not his wife.

Brutus. You are my true and honourable wife,
  As dear to me as are the ruddy drops
  That visit my sad heart.   *290*

Portia. If this were true, then should I know this
    secret.
  I grant I am a woman; but withal[137]
  A woman that Lord Brutus took to wife.
  I grant I am a woman; but withal
  A woman well reputed, Cato's daughter.[138]   *295*
  Think you I am no stronger than my sex,
  Being so father'd and so husbanded?
  Tell me your counsels,[139] I will not disclose 'em.
  I have made strong proof of my constancy,
  Giving myself a voluntary wound   *300*
  Here, in the thigh. Can I bear that with patience,
  And not my husband's secrets?

---

[132] *excepted*: an exception (to their union).

[133] *in sort or limitation*: in a manner or with certain legal restrictions.

[134] *keep*: be.

[135] *comfort*: give joy to.

[136] *suburbs*: outlying districts (where taverns and brothels were usually located).

[137] *withal*: with that.

[138] *Cato's daughter*: Marcus Porcius Cato (Cato the Younger; 95–46 B.C.), an ally of Pompey against Caesar, was Brutus' uncle and father-in-law.

[139] *counsels*: secrets, deepest concerns.

Brutus. O ye gods,
  Render me worthy of this noble wife!

[*Knocking within.*]

Hark, hark! one knocks. Portia, go in awhile,
And by and by thy bosom shall partake   *305*
The secrets of my heart.
All my engagements[140] I will construe[141] to thee,
All the charactery of[142] my sad brows.
Leave me with haste.   [*Exit Portia.*]
          Lucius, who's that knocks?

Enter Lucius and Ligarius.

Lucius. Here is a sick man that would speak with
  you.   *310*

Brutus. Caius Ligarius, that Metellus spake of.
  Boy, stand aside. Caius Ligarius, how?[143]

Ligarius. Vouchsafe[144] good morrow from a feeble
  tongue.

Brutus. O, what a time have you chose out,
    brave[145] Caius,
  To wear a kerchief![146] Would you were not sick!   *315*

Ligarius. I am not sick, if Brutus have in hand
  Any exploit worthy the name of honour.

Brutus. Such an exploit have I in hand, Ligarius,
  Had you a healthful ear to hear of it.

---

[140] *engagements*: commitments, sworn plans.

[141] *construe*: explain.

[142] *charactery of*: the character or feelings expressed in.

[143] *how?* how are you?

[144] *Vouchsafe*: please accept.

[145] *brave*: noble.

[146] *kerchief*: shawl (associated with invalids) worn about the head to protect against drafts.

Ligarius. By all the gods that Romans bow
    before,   320
  I here discard my sickness. [*Pulls off his*
  kerchief] Soul of Rome!
  Brave son, deriv'd from honourable loins![147]
  Thou, like an exorcist,[148] hast conjur'd up
  My mortified[149] spirit. Now bid me run,
  And I will strive with things impossible;   325
  Yea, get the better of them. What's to do?

Brutus. A piece of work that will make sick men
    whole.

Ligarius. But are not some whole that we must
    make sick?

Brutus. That must we also. What it is, my Caius,
  I shall unfold to thee, as we are going   330
  To whom[150] it must be done.

Ligarius.   Set on[151] your foot,
  And with a heart new-fir'd I follow you
  To do I know not what; but it sufficeth
  That Brutus leads me on.   [*Thunder.*]

Brutus.   Follow me, then.

                         [*Exeunt.*]

---

[147] *deriv'd from honourable loins*: i.e., descended from Lucius Junius Brutus.
[148] *exorcist*: conjurer.
[149] *mortified*: deadened.
[150] *To whom*: to the home of him to whom.
[151] *Set on*: advance, move forward.

Scene 2. Rome. Caesar's house.

Thunder and lightning. Enter Julius Caesar in his night-gown.[152]

Caesar. Nor heaven nor earth have been at peace
　　to-night.
　Thrice hath Calphurnia in her sleep cried out
　'Help, ho! They murder Caesar!' Who's within?

Enter a Servant.

Servant. My lord?

Caesar. Go bid the priests do present[153] sacrifice,　　5
　And bring me their opinions of success.[154]

Servant. I will, my lord.　　　　　　　　[Exit.]

Enter Calphurnia.

Calphurnia. What mean you, Caesar? Think you to
　　walk forth?
　You shall not stir out of your house to-day.

Caesar. Caesar shall forth; the things that
　　threaten'd me　　　　　　　　　　　　　　10
　Ne'er look'd but on my back. When they shall
　　see
　The face of Caesar, they are vanished.

Calphurnia. Caesar, I never stood on
　　ceremonies,[155]
　Yet now they fright me. There is one within,
　Besides the things that we have heard and seen,　　15

---

[152] *night-gown*: dressing gown.

[153] *present*: immediate.

[154] *opinions of success*: result of their sacrifices (good or bad).

[155] *stood on ceremonies*: believed in the interpretation of omens.

Recounts most horrid sights seen by the watch.[156]
A lioness hath whelped[157] in the streets,
And graves have yawn'd[158] and yielded up their
    dead;
Fierce fiery warriors fight upon the clouds,
In ranks and squadrons and right form of war,[159]   20
Which drizzled blood upon the Capitol;
The noise of battle hurtled[160] in the air;
Horses did neigh, and dying men did groan,
And ghosts did shriek and squeal about the
    streets.
O Caesar, these things are beyond all use,[161]   25
And I do fear them!

Caesar.   What can be avoided,
    Whose end is purpos'd by the mighty gods?
    Yet Caesar shall go forth; for these predictions
    Are to[162] the world in general as to Caesar.

Calphurnia. When beggars die there are no
        comets seen: 30
    The heavens themselves blaze forth[163] the death of
        princes.

Caesar. Cowards die many times before their
        deaths:
    The valiant never taste of death but once.
    Of all the wonders that I yet have heard,
    It seems to me most strange that men should
        fear,   35

---

[156] *watch*: night watchmen.
[157] *whelped*: given birth to a cub.
[158] *yawn'd*: gaped, opened.
[159] *right form of war*: proper battle formation.
[160] *hurtled*: rushed.
[161] *all use*: usual experience.
[162] *Are to*: apply to.
[163] *blaze forth*: proclaim, signal.

Seeing that death, a necessary end,
Will come when it will come.

Re-enter Servant.

                              What say the augurers?

Servant. They would not have you to stir forth
    to-day.
    Plucking the entrails of an offering forth,
    They could not find a heart within the beast.   40

Caesar. The gods do this in shame of cowardice.
    Caesar should[164] be a beast without a heart,[165]
    If he should stay at home to-day for fear.
    No, Caesar shall not. Danger knows full well
    That Caesar is more dangerous than he: 45
    We are two lions litter'd in one day,
    And I the elder and more terrible;
    And Caesar shall go forth.

Calphurnia.   Alas, my lord,
    Your wisdom is consum'd in confidence.[166]
    Do not go forth to-day. Call it my fear   50
    That keeps you in the house, and not your own.
    We'll send Mark Antony to the Senate House,
    And he shall say you are not well to-day.
    Let me, upon my knee, prevail in this.

Caesar. Mark Antony shall say I am not well;   55
    And for thy humour[167] I will stay at home.

Enter Decius.

Here's Decius Brutus, he shall tell them so.

---

[164] *should:* would truly.
[165] *heart:* organ wherein courage is figuratively believed to be lodged.
[166] *consum'd in confidence:* influenced by overconfidence.
[167] *humour:* whim, good humor, preference.

Decius. Caesar, all hail! Good morrow, worthy
   Caesar.
   I come to fetch[168] you to the Senate House.

Caesar. And you are come in very happy[169] time,   60
   To bear my greeting to the senators
   And tell them that I will not come to-day.
   Cannot, is false; and that I dare not, falser;
   I will not come to-day. Tell them so, Decius.

Calphurnia. Say he is sick.

Caesar.   Shall Caesar send a lie?   65
   Have I in conquest stretch'd mine arm so far,
   To be afeard to tell greybeards the truth?
   Decius, go tell them, Caesar will not come.

Decius. Most mighty Caesar, let me know some
   cause,
   Lest I be laugh'd at when I tell them so.   70

Caesar. The cause is in my will: I will not come.
   That is enough to satisfy the Senate.
   But for your private satisfaction,
   Because I love you, I will let you know:
   Calphurnia here, my wife, stays[170] me at home.   75
   She dreamt to-night[171] she saw my statue,[172]
   Which, like a fountain with an hundred spouts,
   Did run pure blood; and many lusty Romans
   Came smiling and did bathe their hands in it.
   And these does she apply for[173] warnings and
   portents   80

[168] *fetch*: escort, bring.
[169] *happy*: opportune, favorable.
[170] *stays*: would keep.
[171] *to-night*: last night.
[172] *statue*: pronounced "statua".
[173] *apply for*: interpret as.

And evils imminent, and on her knee
Hath begg'd that I will stay at home to-day.

Decius. This dream is all amiss interpreted;
    It was a vision fair and fortunate.
    Your statue spouting blood in many pipes,   85
    In which so many smiling Romans bath'd,
    Signifies that from you great Rome shall suck
    Reviving blood, and that great men shall press
    For tinctures,[174] stains,[175] relics,[176] and cognizance.[177]
    This by Calphurnia's dream is signified.   90

Caesar. And this way have you well expounded
    it.

Decius. I have, when you have heard what I can
      say—
    And know it now: the Senate have concluded
    To give this day a crown to mighty Caesar.
    If you shall send them word you will not come,   95
    Their minds may change. Besides, it were a
      mock
    Apt to be render'd,[178] for some one to say
    'Break up the Senate till another time,
    When Caesar's wife shall meet with better
      dreams'.
    If Caesar hide himself, shall they not whisper   100
    'Lo, Caesar is afraid'?
    Pardon me, Caesar; for my dear dear love
    To your proceeding[179] bids me tell you this,
    And reason to my love is liable.[180]

---

[174] tinctures: metals used in heraldry.

[175] stains: colors in heraldry.

[176] relics: sacred tokens of a martyr (possibly stained by his blood).

[177] cognizance: emblems worn to identify a nobleman's retainers.

[178] mock / Apt to be render'd: joke likely to be made.

[179] proceeding: (1) advancement; (2) goals.

[180] reason to my love is liable: my affections rule my judgment.

Caesar. How foolish do your fears seem now,
    Calphurnia!   *105*
  I am ashamed I did yield to them.
  Give me my robe,[181] for I will go.

Enter Brutus, Ligarius, Metellus, Casca, Trebonius,
Cinna, and Publius.

  And look where Publius is come to fetch me.

Publius. Good morrow, Caesar.

Caesar.   Welcome, Publius.
  What, Brutus, are you stirr'd so early too?   *110*
  Good morrow, Casca. Caius Ligarius,
  Caesar was ne'er so much your enemy[182]
  As that same ague[183] which hath made you lean.
  What is't o'clock?

Brutus.   Caesar, 'tis strucken eight.

Caesar. I thank you for your pains and courtesy.

Enter Antony.   *115*

  See! Antony, that revels long o' nights,
  Is notwithstanding up. Good morrow, Antony.

Antony. So to most noble Caesar.

Caesar.   Bid them prepare within.
  I am to blame to be thus waited for.
  Now, Cinna. Now, Metellus. What, Trebonius!
  I have an hour's talk in store for you.   *120*
  Remember that you call on me to-day;
  Be near me, that I may remember you.

---

[181] *robe*: i.e., toga.
[182] *enemy*: Ligarius sided against Caesar in the recent civil war that led to the
latter's ascendency.
[183] *ague*: illness involving fever and shivering (examples include malaria).

Trebonius. Caesar, I will. [*Aside*] And so near
    will I be,
  That your best friends shall wish I had been
    further.

Caesar. Good friends, go in and taste some wine   *125*
    with me;
  And we, like friends, will straightway go
    together.

Brutus. [*Aside*] That every like is not the same,[184]
    O Caesar,
  The heart of Brutus earns[185] to think upon!

                          [*Exeunt.*]

Scene 3. *Rome. A street near the Capitol.*

Enter Artemidorus reading a paper.

Artemidorus. 'Caesar, beware of Brutus; take
  heed of Cassius; come not near Casca; have an
  eye to Cinna; trust not Trebonius; mark well
  Metellus Cimber; Decius Brutus loves thee not;
  thou hast wrong'd Caius Ligarius. There is but
  one mind in all these men, and it is bent against[186]
  Caesar. If thou beest not immortal, look about
  you. Security gives way to conspiracy.[187] The   5
  mighty gods defend thee!
                 Thy lover,[188]

                        ARTEMIDORUS.'

Here will I stand till Caesar pass along,

---

[184] *That every like is not the same:* I.e., it is a pity that those who appear to be friends may in fact be enemies.

[185] *earns:* (1) yearns; (2) grieves.

[186] *bent against:* directed toward.

[187] *Security gives way to conspiracy:* overconfidence opens the door to conspiracy.

[188] *lover:* devoted friend.

And as a suitor[189] will I give him this.
My heart laments that virtue cannot live   *10*
Out of the teeth of emulation.[190]
If thou read this, O, Caesar, thou mayest live;
If not, the fates with traitors do contrive.[191]

                                        [*Exit.*]

Scene 4. *Rome. Before the house of Brutus.*

Enter Portia and Lucius.

Portia. I prithee, boy, run to the Senate House.
    Stay not to answer me, but get thee gone.
    Why dost thou stay?

Lucius.   To know my errand, madam.

Portia. I would have had thee there and here
        again,
    Ere I can tell thee what thou shouldst do there.   *5*
    [*Aside*] O constancy,[192] be strong upon my side!
    Set a huge mountain 'tween my heart and
        tongue!
    I have a man's mind, but a woman's might.[193]
    How hard it is for women to keep counsel!—
    Art thou here yet?

Lucius.   Madam, what should I do?   *10*
    Run to the Capitol, and nothing else?
    And so return to you, and nothing else?

---

[189] *as a suitor*: like a petitioner.
[190] *Out of the teeth of emulation*: beyond the reach (bite) of envious rivalry.
[191] *contrive*: scheme, conspire.
[192] *constancy*: resolution.
[193] *might*: physical strength.

Portia. Yes, bring me word, boy, if thy lord look
     well,
   For he went sickly forth; and take good note
   What Caesar doth, what suitors press to him.   15
   Hark, boy! What noise is that?

Lucius. I hear none, madam.

Portia.   Prithee listen well.
   I heard a bustling rumour,[194] like a fray,
   And the wind brings it from the Capitol.

Lucius. Sooth,[195] madam, I hear nothing.

Enter the Soothsayer.

Portia.   Come hither, fellow.   20
   Which way hast thou been?

Soothsayer.   At mine own house, good lady.

Portia. What is't o'clock?

Soothsayer.   About the ninth hour, lady.

Portia. Is Caesar yet gone to the Capitol?

Soothsayer. Madam, not yet. I go to take my
     stand,   25
   To see him pass on to the Capitol.

Portia. Thou hast some suit to Caesar, hast thou
     not?

Soothsayer. That I have, lady. If it will please
     Caesar
   To be so good to Caesar as to hear me,
   I shall beseech him to befriend himself.

---

[194] *rumour:* outcry (like in battle).
[195] *Sooth:* truly.

Portia. Why, know'st thou any harm's intended
    towards him?   30

Soothsayer. None that I know will be, much
    that I fear may chance.[196]
  Good morrow to you. Here the street is narrow;
  The throng that follows Caesar at the heels,
  Of senators, of praetors,[197] common suitors,
  Will crowd a feeble man almost to death.   35
  I'll get me to a place more void,[198] and there
  Speak to great Caesar as he comes along.

                                            [*Exit.*]

Portia. I must go in. [Aside] Ay me, how weak a
    thing
  The heart of woman is! O Brutus,
  The heavens speed thee in thine enterprise!   40
  Sure the boy heard me.—Brutus hath a suit
  That Caesar will not grant.—O, I grow faint.—
  Run, Lucius, and commend me[199] to my lord;
  Say I am merry.[200] Come to me again,
  And bring me word what he doth say to thee.   45

                              [*Exeunt severally.*[201]]

---

[196] *chance*: come to be.
[197] *praetors*: elected magistrates (Brutus was *praetor urbanus*, the chief justice).
[198] *more void*: less crowded with people.
[199] *commend me*: give my greetings and goodwill.
[200] *merry*: cheerful, even frivolously so.
[201] *severally*: separately.

ACT 3

Scene 1. *Rome. A street before the Capitol.*

Flourish. Enter Caesar, Brutus, Cassius, Casca, Decius,
Metellus, Trebonius, Cinna, Antony, Lepidus,
Artemidorus, Popilius, Publius, and the Soothsayer.

Caesar. The ides of March are come.

Soothsayer. Ay, Caesar, but not gone.

Artemidorus. Hail, Caesar! Read this schedule.[1]

Decius. Trebonius doth desire you to o'er-read,
At your best leisure, this his humble suit.   5

Artemidorus. O Caesar, read mine first; for
     mine's a suit
That touches Caesar nearer. Read it, great
     Caesar.

Caesar. What touches us ourself shall be last
serv'd.[2]

Artemidorus. Delay not, Caesar; read it
     instantly.

Caesar. What, is the fellow mad?

Publius.   Sirrah,[3] give place.[4]   10

Cassius. What, urge you your petitions in the
     street?
Come to the Capitol.

Caesar enters the Capitol, the rest following.

---

[1] *schedule*: scroll.
[2] *serv'd*: presented, delivered (legal term, as in a legal writ or other document).
[3] *Sirrah*: term of address to inferiors.
[4] *give place*: move, give up your place.

Popilius. I wish your enterprise to-day may
        thrive.

Cassius. What enterprise, Popilius?

Popilius.   Fare you well.

                        [*Advances to Caesar.*]

Brutus. What said Popilius Lena?   15

Cassius. He wish'd to-day our enterprise might
        thrive.
    I fear our purpose is discovered.

Brutus. Look how he makes to[5] Caesar. Mark
        him.

Cassius. Casca, be sudden,[6] for we fear
        prevention.[7]
    Brutus, what shall be done? If this be known,   20
    Cassius or Caesar never shall turn back,[8]
    For I will slay myself.

Brutus.   Cassius, be constant.[9]
    Popilius Lena speaks not of our purposes;
    For look, he smiles, and Caesar doth not
        change.[10]

Cassius. Trebonius knows his time; for look you,
        Brutus,   25
    He draws Mark Antony out of the way.

                    [*Exeunt Antony and Trebonius.*]

---

[5] *makes to*: heads toward.

[6] *sudden*: swift.

[7] *prevention*: being forestalled.

[8] *Cassius or Caesar never shall turn back*: I.e., either Cassius or Caesar will die.

[9] *constant*: (1) calm; (2) resolved in purpose.

[10] *change*: i.e., change in his expression or appearance (he is not enraged or appalled).

Decius. Where is Metellus Cimber? Let him go
  And presently prefer[11] his suit to Caesar.

Brutus. He is address'd;[12] press near and second
  him.

Cinna. Casca, you are the first that rears your
  hand.   30

Caesar. Are we all ready? What is now amiss
  That Caesar and his Senate must redress?

Metellus. Most high, most mighty, and most
      puissant[13] Caesar,
  Metellus Cimber throws before thy seat
  An humble heart.   [*Kneeling.*]

Caesar.   I must prevent thee, Cimber.   35
  These couchings[14] and these lowly[15] courtesies
  Might fire the blood of ordinary men,
  And turn pre-ordinance and first decree[16]
  Into the law of children. Be not fond[17]
  To think that Caesar bears such rebel blood[18]   40
  That will be thaw'd from the true[19] quality[20]
  With that which melteth fools—I mean, sweet
      words,
  Low-crooked curtsies, and base spaniel[21] fawning.
  Thy brother by decree is banished;
  If thou dost bend, and pray, and fawn for him,   45

[11] *presently prefer*: at once, immediately present.
[12] *address'd*: ready, prepared.
[13] *puissant*: powerful, influential.
[14] *couchings*: crouching, bowing protestations.
[15] *lowly*: (1) humble; (2) abasing.
[16] *pre-ordinance and first decree*: ancient customs or laws.
[17] *fond*: foolish enough.
[18] *rebel blood*: uncontrolled, rebellious blood (feelings).
[19] *true*: proper.
[20] *quality*: (1) character; (2) degree of excellence.
[21] *spaniel*: breed of dog with drooping ears, known for its blind obedience.

I spurn thee like a cur out of my way.
Know, Caesar doth not wrong; nor without
   cause
Will he be satisfied.

Metellus. Is there no voice more worthy than
   my own
To sound more sweetly in great Caesar's ear   50
For the repealing[22] of my banish'd brother?

Brutus. I kiss thy hand, but not in flattery,
   Caesar,
Desiring thee that Publius Cimber may
Have an immediate freedom of repeal.

Caesar. What, Brutus!

Cassius.   Pardon, Caesar! Caesar, pardon!   55
As low as to thy foot doth Cassius fall,
To beg enfranchisement[23] for Publius Cimber.

Caesar. I could be well mov'd, if I were as you;
If I could pray to move,[24] prayers would move me;
But I am constant as the northern star,[25]   60
Of whose true-fix'd and resting[26] quality
There is no fellow[27] in the firmament.
The skies are painted with unnumb'red[28] sparks,
They are all fire, and every one doth shine;
But there's but one in all doth hold[29] his place.   65
So in the world: 'tis furnish'd well with men,
And men are flesh and blood, and apprehensive;[30]

---

[22] *repealing*: recalling, bringing back (from banishment).
[23] *enfranchisement*: freedom, restoration to the proper rights of a citizen.
[24] *move*: i.e., sway or influence the opinions or decisions of others.
[25] *northern star*: Polaris, the polestar, used as a point of navigation.
[26] *resting*: changeless, having constancy of character.
[27] *fellow*: equal.
[28] *unnumb'red*: innumerable, uncountable.
[29] *hold*: hold to, keep to.
[30] *apprehensive*: capable of reason or perception.

Yet in the number I do know but one
That unassailable holds on his rank,
Unshak'd of motion; and that I am he,   70
Let me a little show it, even in this—
That I was constant[31] Cimber should be banish'd,
And constant do remain to keep him so.

Cinna. O Caesar!

Caesar.   Hence! Wilt thou lift up Olympus?[32]

Decius. Great Caesar!

Caesar.   Doth not Brutus bootless[33] kneel?   75

Casca. Speak, hands, for me!

[*They stab Caesar. Casca strikes the first, Brutus the last blow.*]

Caesar. Et tu, Brute?[34]—Then fall, Caesar!

[*Dies.*]

Cinna. Liberty! Freedom! Tyranny is dead!
   Run hence, proclaim, cry it about the streets.

Cassius. Some to the common pulpits,[35] and cry
      out   80
   'Liberty, freedom, and enfranchisement!'

Brutus. People and Senators, be not affrighted.
   Fly not; stand still. Ambition's debt is paid.[36]

Casca. Go to the pulpit, Brutus.

Decius. And Cassius too.   85

---

[31] *constant:* determined.
[32] *Olympus:* mountain in Thessaly that is the abode of the gods in classical mythology.
[33] *bootless:* in vain.
[34] *Et tu, Brute?* And you (too), Brutus? (Latin).
[35] *pulpits:* speaker's stands.
[36] *Ambition's debt is paid:* Caesar's ambition has received its just deserts.

Brutus. Where's Publius?

Cinna. Here, quite confounded with this mutiny.[37]

Metellus. Stand fast together, lest some friend of
    Caesar's
  Should chance—

Brutus. Talk not of standing.[38] Publius, good
    cheer!   90
  There is no harm intended to your person,
  Nor to no Roman else. So tell them, Publius.

Cassius. And leave us, Publius, lest that the
    people,
  Rushing on us, should do your age some
    mischief.

Brutus. Do so; and let no man abide[39] this deed   95
  But we the doers.

Re-enter Trebonius.

Cassius. Where is Antony?

Trebonius.   Fled to his house amaz'd.[40]
  Men, wives, and children, stare, cry out, and
    run,
  As[41] it were doomsday.

Brutus.   Fates,[42] we will know your pleasures.
  That we shall die, we know; 'tis but the time,   100
  And drawing days out, that men stand upon.[43]

---

[37] *confounded with this mutiny*: overwhelmed by all the tumult.

[38] *standing*: organizing, planning out a stance.

[39] *abide*: bear the consequences of.

[40] *amaz'd*: confused, dismayed.

[41] *As*: as if.

[42] *Fates*: in classical mythology, three goddesses who ruled over the lives of men.

[43] *stand upon*: strive, hope for.

Cassius. Why, he that cuts off twenty years of life
  Cuts off so many years of fearing death.

Brutus. Grant that, and then is death a benefit.
  So are we Caesar's friends, that have abridg'd   105
  His time of fearing death. Stoop, Romans, stoop,
  And let us bathe our hands in Caesar's blood
  Up to the elbows, and besmear our swords.
  Then walk we forth, even to the marketplace,[44]
  And waving our red weapons o'er our heads,   110
  Let's all cry 'Peace, freedom, and liberty!'

Cassius. Stoop then, and wash. How many ages
      hence
  Shall this our lofty scene be acted over
  In states unborn and accents[45] yet unknown!

Brutus. How many times shall Caesar bleed in
      sport,[46]   115
  That now on Pompey's basis[47] lies along[48]
  No worthier than the dust!

Cassius.   So oft as that shall be,
  So often shall the knot[49] of us be call'd
  The men that gave their country liberty.

Decius. What, shall we forth?

Cassius.   Ay, every man away.   120
  Brutus shall lead, and we will grace his heels
  With the most boldest[50] and best hearts of Rome.

Enter a Servant.

---

[44] *marketplace*: the Roman Forum, the center of Roman public life.
[45] *accents*: languages.
[46] *in sport*: as part of a public entertainment.
[47] *Pompey's basis*: base of the pedestal of the statue of Pompey.
[48] *along*: stretched out at full length.
[49] *knot*: close group.
[50] *most boldest*: an emphatic superlative.

Brutus. Soft,[51] who comes here? A friend of
    Antony's.

Servant. Thus, Brutus, did my master bid me
    kneel;
    Thus did Mark Antony bid me fall down;   *125*
    And, being prostrate, thus he bade me say:
    Brutus is noble, wise, valiant, and honest;
    Caesar was mighty, bold, royal,[52] and loving.
    Say I love Brutus, and I honour him;
    Say I fear'd Caesar, honour'd him, and lov'd
      him.   *130*
    If Brutus will vouchsafe that Antony
    May safely come to him, and be resolv'd[53]
    How Caesar hath deserv'd to lie in death,
    Mark Antony shall not love Caesar dead
    So well as Brutus living; but will follow   *135*
    The fortunes and affairs of noble Brutus
    Thorough[54] the hazards of this untrod state[55]
    With all true faith. So says my master Antony.

Brutus. Thy master is a wise and valiant Roman;
    I never thought him worse.   *140*
    Tell him, so[56] please him come unto this place,
    He shall be satisfied and, by my honour,
    Depart untouch'd.

Servant.   I'll fetch him presently.[57]

                                   [*Exit.*]

---

[51] *Soft*: wait.
[52] *royal*: princely, beneficent.
[53] *be resolv'd*: know for certain.
[54] *Thorough*: through.
[55] *untrod state*: unknown, new state of affairs.
[56] *so*: if he.
[57] *presently*: immediately.

Brutus. I know that we shall have him well to
    friend.[58]

Cassius. I wish we may. But yet have I a mind   *145*
    That fears him much; and my misgiving still
    Falls shrewdly to the purpose.[59]

Re-enter Antony.

Brutus. But here comes Antony. Welcome,
    Mark Antony.

Antony. O mighty Caesar! dost thou lie so low?
    Are all thy conquests, glories, triumphs, spoils,   *150*
    Shrunk to this little measure? Fare thee well.
    I know not, gentlemen, what you intend,
    Who else must be let blood,[60] who else is rank.[61]
    If I myself, there is no hour so fit
    As Caesar's death's hour; nor no instrument   *155*
    Of half that worth as those your swords, made
        rich
    With the most noble blood of all this world.
    I do beseech ye, if you bear me hard,[62]
    Now, whilst your purpled[63] hands do reek and
        smoke,[64]
    Fulfil your pleasure. Live[65] a thousand years,   *160*
    I shall not find myself so apt[66] to die.
    No place will please me so, no mean[67] of death,

---

[58] *well to friend*: (1) as a good friend; (2) well worth befriending.

[59] *my misgiving . . . to the purpose*: my astute and serious concerns continue to
be insightful regarding the real situation.

[60] *let blood*: (1) purified (as in "letting blood", a medical practice widely used
at the time, through which unwholesome elements were supposed to be purified
from the body); (2) killed.

[61] *rank*: diseased and swollen (in need of bloodletting).

[62] *bear me hard*: bear ill will toward me.

[63] *purpled*: i.e., stained with blood (and royal blood at that).

[64] *reek and smoke*: steam (with fresh blood).

[65] *Live*: though I may live.

[66] *apt*: prepared, ready.

[67] *mean*: means, manner.

As here by Caesar, and by you cut off,
The choice and master spirits of this age.

Brutus. O Antony! beg not your death of us.   165
  Though now we must appear bloody and cruel,
  As by our hands and this our present act
  You see we do; yet see you but our hands,
  And this the bleeding business they have done.
  Our hearts you see not; they are pitiful;[68]   170
  And pity to the general wrong of Rome,
  As fire drives out fire, so pity pity,[69]
  Hath done this deed on Caesar. For your part,
  To you our swords have leaden[70] points, Mark
      Antony;
  Our arms in strength of malice,[71] and our hearts   175
  Of brothers' temper,[72] do receive you in
  With all kind love, good thoughts, and
      reverence.

Cassius. Your voice[73] shall be as strong as any man's
  In the disposing of new dignities.[74]

Brutus. Only be patient till we have appeas'd   180
  The multitude, beside themselves with fear,
  And then we will deliver you[75] the cause
  Why I, that did love Caesar when I struck him,
  Have thus proceeded.

Antony.   I doubt not of your wisdom.
  Let each man render me his bloody hand.   185

---

[68] *pitiful*: full of pity.

[69] *pity pity*: I.e., the pity for the situation of Rome drove out any pity for Caesar.

[70] *leaden*: i.e., blunt.

[71] *Our arms in strength of malice*: our use of weapons is motivated by feelings of anger.

[72] *our hearts / Of brothers' temper*: we feel like brothers in our hearts.

[73] *voice*: particularly as a vote in the Senate.

[74] *In the disposing of new dignities*: in dividing offices of government after Caesar's death.

[75] *deliver you*: explain to you.

First, Marcus Brutus, will I shake with you;
Next, Caius Cassius, do I take your hand;
Now, Decius Brutus, yours; now yours,
    Metellus;
Yours, Cinna; and, my valiant Casca, yours.
Though last, not least in love, yours, good
    Trebonius.   190
Gentlemen all—alas, what shall I say?
My credit[76] now stands on such slippery ground
That one of two bad ways you must conceit[77] me,
Either a coward or a flatterer.
That I did love thee, Caesar, O, 'tis true!   195
If then thy spirit look upon us now,
Shall it not grieve thee dearer[78] than thy death
To see thy Antony making his peace,
Shaking the bloody fingers of thy foes,
Most noble! in the presence of thy corse?[79]
Had I as many eyes as thou hast wounds,   200
Weeping as fast as they stream forth thy blood,
It would become me better than to close[80]
In terms of friendship with thine enemies.
Pardon me, Julius! Here wast thou bay'd,[81] brave
    hart;[82]
Here didst thou fall; and here thy hunters stand,   205
Sign'd in thy spoil,[83] and crimson'd in thy lethe.[84]
O world, thou wast the forest to this hart;

[76] *credit*: credibility, reputation.
[77] *conceit*: judge, conceive of.
[78] *dearer*: more dearly, keenly.
[79] *corse*: corpse.
[80] *close*: join, ally oneself.
[81] *bay'd*: brought to bay (like an animal).
[82] *hart*: stag (a noble animal, also a pun on "heart").
[83] *spoil*: blood.
[84] *lethe*: life's blood. (In classical mythology, Lethe is the river of the dead of the realm of Hades, the water of which, when drunk, causes the dead to forget their lives on earth. The term is also used for the gore of dead animals, with which hunters traditionally smeared themselves.)

And this indeed, O world, the heart of thee!
How like a deer strucken[85] by many princes   *210*
Dost thou here lie!

Cassius. Mark Antony—

Antony.   Pardon me, Caius Cassius.
The enemies of Caesar shall say this;
Then, in a friend, it is cold modesty.[86]

Cassius. I blame you not for praising Caesar so;   *215*
But what compact mean you to have with us?
Will you be prick'd[87] in number of our friends,
Or shall we on,[88] and not depend on you?

Antony. Therefore I took your hands; but was
     indeed
Sway'd from the point by looking down on
     Caesar.   *220*
Friends am I with you all, and love you all,
Upon this hope, that you shall give me reasons
Why and wherein Caesar was dangerous.

Brutus. Or else were this[89] a savage spectacle.
Our reasons are so full of good regard[90]   *225*
That were you, Antony, the son of Caesar,
You should be satisfied.

Antony.   That's all I seek;
And am moreover suitor that I may
Produce[91] his body to the market-place

---

[85] *strucken:* stricken, struck down, killed.
[86] *modesty:* moderation.
[87] *prick'd:* counted, marked down (in a tally of the number of friends).
[88] *on:* go on.
[89] *were this:* this would be.
[90] *regard:* consideration, reasoning.
[91] *Produce:* present, bring forth.

And, in the pulpit, as becomes a friend,   *230*
Speak in the order[92] of his funeral.

Brutus. You shall, Mark Antony.

Cassius.   Brutus, a word with you.
[*Aside to Brutus*] You know not what you do.
    Do not consent
That Antony speak in his funeral.
Know you how much the people may be mov'd   *235*
By that which he will utter?

Brutus. [*Aside to Cassius*] By your pardon—
I will myself into the pulpit first,
And show the reason of our Caesar's death.
What Antony shall speak, I will protest[93]
He speaks by leave and by permission;   *240*
And that we are contented Caesar shall
Have all true rites and lawful ceremonies.
It shall advantage[94] more than do us wrong.[95]

Cassius. I know not what may fall.[96] I like it not.

Brutus. Mark Antony, here, take you Caesar's
    body.   *245*
You shall not in your funeral speech blame us,
But speak all good you can devise of Caesar;
And say you do't by our permission;
Else shall you not have any hand at all
About his funeral. And you shall speak   *250*
In the same pulpit whereto I am going,
After my speech is ended.

Antony.   Be it so;
I do desire no more.

---

[92] *order*: course of a ceremony.
[93] *protest*: declare, explain.
[94] *advantage*: be to the benefit of.
[95] *wrong*: harm.
[96] *fall*: befall, happen.

Brutus. Prepare the body then, and follow us.

[*Exeunt all but Antony.*]

Antony. O, pardon me, thou bleeding piece of   255
    earth,[97]
  That I am meek and gentle with these butchers!
  Thou art the ruins of the noblest man
  That ever lived in the tide of times.[98]
  Woe to the hand that shed this costly blood!
  Over thy wounds now do I prophesy—   260
  Which like dumb[99] mouths do ope[100] their ruby lips
  To beg the voice and utterance[101] of my tongue—
  A curse shall light upon the limbs of men;
  Domestic[102] fury and fierce civil strife
  Shall cumber[103] all the parts of Italy;   265
  Blood and destruction shall be so in use,[104]
  And dreadful objects so familiar,
  That mothers shall but smile when they behold
  Their infants quartered with the hands of war,
  All pity chok'd with custom of fell[105] deeds;   270
  And Caesar's spirit, ranging for revenge,
  With Até[106] by his side come hot from hell,
  Shall in these confines[107] with a monarch's voice
  Cry 'Havoc!'[108] and let slip[109] the dogs of war,

---

[97] *piece of earth*: i.e., man (formed from the earth).

[98] *tide of times*: the ebb and flow of the stream of history.

[99] *dumb*: mute.

[100] *ope*: open.

[101] *utterance*: (1) speech; (2) vehemence.

[102] *Domestic*: i.e., internal, national.

[103] *cumber*: encumber, oppress.

[104] *in use*: customary, widely experienced.

[105] *fell*: cruel.

[106] *Até*: in classical mythology, goddess of discord and vengeance.

[107] *in these confines*: within these boundaries, this region.

[108] *Havoc!* the order for unrestrained slaughter in a battle (which only the king could give).

[109] *let slip*: unleash.

That this foul deed shall smell above the earth   *275*
With carrion[110] men, groaning for burial.

Enter Octavius' Servant.

You serve Octavius Caesar, do you not?

Servant. I do, Mark Antony.

Antony. Caesar did write for him to come to
    Rome.

Servant. He did receive his letters, and is
    coming,   *280*
And bid me say to you by word of mouth—
O Caesar!   [*Seeing the body.*]

Antony. Thy heart is big,[111] get thee apart and
    weep.
Passion,[112] I see, is catching; for mine eyes,
Seeing those beads of sorrow stand in thine,   *285*
Began to water. Is thy master coming?

Servant. He lies to-night within seven leagues of
    Rome.

Antony. Post[113] back with speed, and tell him what
    hath chanc'd.[114]
Here is a mourning Rome, a dangerous Rome,
No Rome[115] of safety for Octavius yet;   *290*
Hie[116] hence and tell him so. Yet stay awhile;
Thou shall not back till I have borne this corse
to the market-place. There shall I try,[117]

---

[110] *carrion*: dead, rotting, needing burial.
[111] *big*: swollen (with grief).
[112] *Passion*: intense emotion (grief).
[113] *Post*: travel swiftly by a relay of horses.
[114] *chanc'd*: happened.
[115] *Rome*: pronounced "room".
[116] *Hie*: hurry.
[117] *try*: test to find out.

In my oration, how the people take
The cruel issue[118] of these bloody men;   295
According to the which thou shalt discourse
To young Octavius of the state of things.
Lend me your hand.

[*Exeunt with Caesar's body.*]

Scene 2. *Rome. The Forum.*

Enter Brutus and Cassius, with the Plebeians.

Citizens. We will be satisfied![119] Let us be satisfied!

Brutus. Then follow me, and give me audience,
    friends.
  Cassius, go you into the other street,
   And part the numbers.[120]
  Those that will hear me speak, let 'em stay here;   5
  Those that will follow Cassius, go with him;
  And public reasons[121] shall be rendered
  Of Caesar's death.

1 Plebeian.   I will hear Brutus speak.

2 Plebeian. I will hear Cassius, and compare
    their reasons,
  When severally we hear them rendered.   10

[*Exit Cassius, with some of the Plebeians. Brutus goes into
the pulpit.*]

3 Plebeian. The noble Brutus is ascended.
    Silence!

---

[118] *cruel issue*: consequences of the cruel actions.
[119] *will be satisfied*: require a full explanation.
[120] *part the numbers*: divide up the crowd.
[121] *public reasons*: (1) publicly given reasons; (2) reasons that touch the public generally.

Brutus. Be patient till the last.[122]
Romans, countrymen, and lovers! hear me for
my cause,[123] and be silent, that you may hear.
Believe me for mine honour,[124] and have respect to[125]
mine honour, that you may believe. Censure[126] me
in your wisdom, and awake your senses,[127] that
you may the better judge. If there be any in this
assembly, any dear friend of Caesar's, to him I
say that Brutus' love to Caesar was no less than
his. If then that friend demand why Brutus rose
against Caesar, this is my answer: Not that I
lov'd Caesar less, but that I lov'd Rome more.
Had you rather Caesar were living, and die all
slaves, than that Caesar were dead, to live all
free men? As Caesar lov'd me, I weep for him; as
he was fortunate, I rejoice at it; as he was
valiant, I honour him; but—as he was
ambitious, I slew him. There is tears for his love;
joy for his fortune; honour for his valour; and
death for his ambition. Who is here so base that
would be a bondman? If any, speak; for him
have I offended. Who is here so rude[128] that would
not be a Roman? If any, speak; for him have I
offended. Who is here so vile that will not love
his country? If any, speak; for him have I
offended. I pause for a reply.

All. None, Brutus, none.

[122] *the last*: the end of the speech.
[123] *my cause*: the cause I defend.
[124] *Believe me for mine honour*: (1) believe in me because you know I am honorable; (2) believe that I am honorable.
[125] *have respect to*: have regard for, remember.
[126] *Censure*: judge, blame.
[127] *senses*: reason.
[128] *rude*: barbarous, rough.

Brutus. Then none have I offended. I have done   35
   no more to Caesar than you shall do to Brutus.[129]
   The question[130] of his death is enroll'd in the
   Capitol; his glory not extenuated,[131] wherein he
   was worthy; nor his offences enforc'd,[132] for which
   he suffered death.

Enter Antony and Others with Caesar's body.

[handwritten: Caesar has power and honor even when dead]

   Here comes his body, mourn'd by Mark Antony,   40
   who, though he had no hand in his death, shall
   receive the benefit of his dying, a place in the
   commonwealth,[133] as which of you shall not? With
   this I depart, that, as I slew my best lover for the
   good of Rome, I have the same dagger for   45
   myself, when it shall please my country to need
   my death.

All. Live, Brutus! live, live! *[handwritten: *rhetoric is powerful]*

1 Plebeian. Bring him with triumph home unto
   his house.

2 Plebeian. Give him a statue with his ancestors.

3 Plebeian. Let him be Caesar.

4 Plebeian.   Caesar's better parts[134]   50
   Shall be crown'd in Brutus.

1 Plebeian. We'll bring him to his house with
   shouts and clamours.

Brutus. My countrymen—

---

[129] *you shall do to Brutus*: i.e., if he became like Caesar.
[130] *question*: (1) subject; (2) reasons, justifications for his death.
[131] *extenuated*: lessened, belittled.
[132] *enforc'd*: exaggerated.
[133] *in the commonwealth*: i.e., as a free Roman citizen with rights.
[134] *parts*: qualities, characteristics.

2 *Plebeian.*   Peace, silence! Brutus speaks.

1 *Plebeian.* Peace, ho!   *emotion is ruling them*

Brutus. Good countrymen, let me depart alone,   55
    And for my sake stay here with Antony.
    Do grace[135] to Caesar's corpse, and grace[136] his speech
    Tending to[137] Caesar's glories, which Mark Antony,
    By our permission, is allow'd to make.
    I do entreat you, not a man depart   60
    Save I alone, till Antony have spoke.   [*Exit.*]

1 *Plebeian.* Stay, ho! and let us hear Mark
    Antony.

3 *Plebeian.* Let him go up into the public chair.
    We'll hear him. Noble Antony, go up.

Antony. For Brutus' sake I am beholding[138] to you.   65

                                    [*Goes up.*]

4 *Plebeian.* What does he say of Brutus?

3 *Plebeian.*   He says, for Brutus' sake
    He finds himself beholding to us all.

4 *Plebeian.* 'Twere best he speak no harm of
    Brutus here.

1 *Plebeian.* This Caesar was a tyrant.

3 *Plebeian.*   Nay, that's certain.
    We are blest that Rome is rid of him.   *confused*   70
                                    ppl

2 *Plebeian.* Peace! let us hear what Antony can
    say.

---

[135] *Do grace*: show honor and respect.
[136] *grace*: show honor and respect to (by listening).
[137] *Tending to*: regarding.
[138] *beholding*: beholden, indebted.

Antony. You gentle Romans—   *pause / upset and drama*

All.   Peace, ho! let us hear him.

Antony. Friends, Romans, countrymen, lend me
        your ears;
    I come to bury Caesar, not to praise him.
    The evil that men do lives after them;   75
    The good is oft interred with their bones;
    So let it be with Caesar. The noble Brutus
    Hath told you Caesar was ambitious.
    If it were so, it was a grievous fault;
    And grievously hath Caesar answer'd it.[139]   80
    Here, under leave of Brutus and the rest—
    For Brutus is an honourable man;   *false*
    So are they all, all honourable men—
    Come I to speak in Caesar's funeral.
    He was my friend, faithful and just to me;   85
    But Brutus says he was ambitious,
    And Brutus is an honourable man.
    He hath brought many captives home to Rome,
    Whose ransoms did the general coffers[140] fill;
    Did this in Caesar seem ambitious?   90
    When that the poor have cried, Caesar hath
        wept;
    Ambition should be made of sterner stuff.
    Yet Brutus says he was ambitious;
    And Brutus is an honourable man.
    You all did see that on the Lupercal   95
    I thrice presented him a kingly crown,
    Which he did thrice refuse. Was this ambition?
    Yet Brutus says he was ambitious;
    And sure he is an honourable man.   *repetition*
    I speak not to disprove what Brutus spoke, *is key* 100
    But here I am to speak what I do know. *in rhetoric*

[139] *answer'd it*: answered for it, been punished for it.
[140] *general coffers*: the treasuries of the republic.

You all did love him once, not without cause;
What cause withholds you, then, to mourn for
   him?
O judgment, thou art fled to brutish beasts,
And men have lost their reason! Bear with me;   *105*
My heart is in the coffin there with Caesar,
And I must pause till it come back to me.   *so sad*

1 Plebeian. Methinks there is much reason in his
   sayings.

2 Plebeian. If thou consider rightly of the matter,
   Caesar has had great wrong.

3 Plebeian.   Has he, masters!   *110*
   I fear there will a worse come in his place.

4 Plebeian. Mark'd ye his words? He would not
   take the crown;
Therefore 'tis certain he was not ambitious.

1 Plebeian. If it be found so, some will dear abide[141]
   it.

2 Plebeian. Poor soul! his eyes are red as fire
   with weeping.   *115*

3 Plebeian. There's not a nobler man in Rome
   than Antony.

4 Plebeian. Now mark him, he begins again to
   speak.

Antony. But yesterday the word of Caesar might
   Have stood against the world: now lies he there,
   And none so poor[142] to do him reverence.   *120*
   O masters, if I were dispos'd to stir
   Your hearts and minds to mutiny and rage,

[141] *dear abide*: keenly suffer the consequences of.
[142] *so poor*: too lowly as.

I should do Brutus wrong, and Cassius wrong,
Who, you all know, are honourable men.
I will not do them wrong; I rather choose   125
To wrong the dead, to wrong myself and you,
Than I will wrong such honourable men.
But here's a parchment with the seal of Caesar;
I found it in his closet[143]—'tis his will.
Let but the commons[144] hear this testament,   130
Which, pardon me, I do not mean to read,
And they would go and kiss dead Caesar's wounds
And dip their napkins[145] in his sacred blood;
Yea, beg a hair of him for memory
And, dying, mention it within their wills,   135
Bequeathing it as a rich legacy
Unto their issue.[146]

4 *Plebeian.* We'll hear the will. Read it, Mark
      Antony.

All. The will, the will! We will hear Caesar's will.

Antony. Have patience, gentle friends, I must not
      read it;   140
   It is not meet you know how Caesar lov'd you.
   You are not wood, you are not stones, but men;
   And being men, hearing the will of Caesar,
   It will inflame you, it will make you mad.
   'Tis good you know not that you are his heirs;   145
   For if you should, O, what would come of it?

4 *Plebeian.* Read the will; we'll hear it, Antony!
   You shall[147] read us the will—Caesar's will.

[143] *closet*: private room, study (perhaps his desk).
[144] *commons*: common people.
[145] *napkins*: handkerchiefs.
[146] *issue*: heirs.
[147] *shall*: must.

Antony. Will you be patient? Will you stay awhile?
   I have o'ershot myself[148] to tell you of it.   150
   I fear I wrong the honourable men
   Whose daggers have stabb'd Caesar; I do fear it.

4 Plebeian. They were traitors. Honourable men!

All. The will! the testament!

2 Plebeian. They were villains, murderers.   155
   The will! Read the will.

Antony. You will compel me, then, to read the
     will?
   Then make a ring about the corpse of Caesar,
   And let me show you him that made the will.
   Shall I descend? and will you give me leave?   160

All. Come down.

2 Plebeian. Descend.   [*Antony comes down.*]

3 Plebeian. You shall have leave.

4 Plebeian. A ring! Stand round.

1 Plebeian. Stand from the hearse, stand from the
   body.

2 Plebeian. Room for Antony, most noble   165
   Antony!

Antony. Nay, press not so upon me; stand far[149] off.

All. Stand back. Room! Bear back.

Antony. If you have tears, prepare to shed them
     now.
   You all do know this mantle.[150] I remember   170
   The first time ever Caesar put it on;

[148] *o'ershot myself*: gone further than I should have or than I intended.
[149] *far*: farther.
[150] *mantle*: cloak, toga.

'Twas on a summer's evening, in his tent,
That day he overcame the Nervii.[151]
Look! in this place ran Cassius' dagger through;
See what a rent the envious[152] Casca made;   *175*
Through this the well-beloved Brutus stabb'd,
And as he pluck'd his cursed steel away,
Mark how the blood of Caesar follow'd it,
As[153] rushing out of doors, to be resolv'd[154]
If Brutus so unkindly[155] knock'd or no;   *180*
For Brutus, as you know, was Caesar's angel.[156]
Judge, O you gods, how dearly Caesar lov'd
  him!
This was the most unkindest[157] cut of all;
For when the noble Caesar saw him stab,
Ingratitude, more strong than traitors' arms,   *185*
Quite vanquish'd him. Then burst his mighty
  heart;
And in his mantle muffling up his face,
Even at the base[158] of Pompey's statue.
Which all the while ran blood, great Caesar fell.
O, what a fall was there, my countrymen!   *190*
Then I, and you, and all of us fell down,
Whilst bloody treason flourish'd[159] over us.
O, now you weep, and I perceive you feel
The dint[160] of pity. These are gracious drops.
Kind souls, what[161] weep you when you but
  behold   *195*

---

[151] *Nervii*: barbarous warrior tribe conquered by Caesar in 57 B.C.
[152] *envious*: spiteful, malevolent.
[153] *As*: as though, as if.
[154] *be resolv'd*: learn certainly, clarify.
[155] *unkindly*: (1) cruelly; (2) unnaturally.
[156] *angel*: (1) guardian angel; (2) dearest friend.
[157] *unkindest*: cruel, unnatural.
[158] *base*: bottom of the pedestal.
[159] *flourish'd*: (1) swaggered, triumphed; (2) brandished a sword.
[160] *dint*: mark left from a stroke or blow.
[161] *what*: (1) why; (2) how much.

Our Caesar's vesture[162] wounded? Look you here,
Here is himself, marr'd as you see with traitors.

1 Plebeian. O piteous spectacle!

2 Plebeian. O noble Caesar!

3 Plebeian. O woeful day!   200

4 Plebeian. O traitors, villains!

1 Plebeian. O most bloody sight!

2 Plebeian. We will be reveng'd.

All. Revenge! About![163] Seek! Burn! Fire! Kill! Slay!
Let not a traitor live!   205

Antony. Stay, countrymen.

1 Plebeian. Peace there! Hear the noble Antony.

2 Plebeian. We'll hear him, we'll follow him,
we'll die with him.

Antony. Good friends, sweet friends, let me not
    stir you up   210
To such a sudden flood of mutiny.
They that have done this deed are honourable.
What private griefs[164] they have, alas, I know not,
That made them do it; they are wise and
    honourable, nope
And will, no doubt, with reasons answer you.   215
I come not, friends, to steal away your hearts; false
I am no orator, as Brutus is,
But, as you know me all, a plain blunt man,
That love my friend; and that they know full
    well

---

[162] *vesture*: clothes.
[163] *About!* Get to it!
[164] *griefs*: grievances, complaints.

That gave me public leave to speak[165] of him. 220
For I have neither wit, nor words, nor worth,
Action, nor utterance, nor the power of speech,
To stir men's blood; I only speak right on.
I tell you that which you yourselves do know;
Show you sweet Caesar's wounds, poor poor
  dumb mouths, 225
And bid them speak for me. But were I Brutus,
And Brutus Antony, there were an Antony
Would ruffle up[166] your spirits, and put a tongue
In every wound of Caesar, that should move
The stones of Rome to rise and mutiny. 230

All. We'll mutiny.

1 Plebeian. We'll burn the house of Brutus.

3 Plebeian. Away, then! Come seek the
  conspirators.

Antony. Yet hear me, countrymen; yet hear me
  speak.

All. Peace, ho! Hear Antony, most noble Antony. 235

Antony. Why, friends, you go to do you know
    not what.
  Wherein hath Caesar thus deserv'd your loves?
  Alas, you know not! I must tell you, then:
  You have forgot the will I told you of.

All. Most true. The will! Let's stay and hear the
    will. 240

Antony. Here is the will, and under Caesar's seal:
  To every Roman citizen he gives,
  To every several[167] man, seventy-five drachmas.[168]

---

[165] *public leave to speak*: (1) permission to speak in public; (2) publicly given permission.
[166] *ruffle up*: rouse to rage.
[167] *several*: individual.
[168] *drachmas*: Greek form of currency.

2 Plebeian. Most noble Caesar! We'll revenge his
   death.

3 Plebeian. O royal Caesar! 245

Antony. Hear me with patience.

All. Peace, ho!

Antony. Moreover, he hath left you all his walks,
   His private arbours, and new-planted orchards,
   On this side Tiber; he hath left them you, 250
   And to your heirs for ever—common pleasures,[169]
   To walk abroad and recreate yourselves.
   Here was a Caesar! When comes such another?

1 Plebeian. Never, never! Come away, away!
   We'll burn his body in the holy place, 255
   And with the brands fire the traitors' houses.
   Take up the body.

2 Plebeian. Go, fetch fire.

3 Plebeian. Pluck down benches.

4 Plebeian. Pluck down forms,[170] windows,[171] any
   thing. [*Exeunt Plebeians with the body.*]

Antony. Now let it work.[172] Mischief, thou art 260
   afoot,
   Take thou what course thou wilt.

Enter a Servant.

                              How now, fellow!

Servant. Sir, Octavius is already come to Rome.

Antony. Where is he?

---

[169] *common pleasures*: public pleasure gardens.

[170] *forms*: long benches.

[171] *windows*: shutters.

[172] *let it work*: I.e., let what he said work (like yeast) upon their imaginations, prompting a social uproar.

Servant. He and Lepidus are at Caesar's house.   265

Antony. And thither will I straight[173] to visit him.
   He comes upon a wish.[174] Fortune is merry,
   And in this mood will give us any thing.

Servant. I heard him say Brutus and Cassius
   Are rid[175] like madmen through the gates of Rome.   270

Antony. Belike[176] they had some notice[177] of the
   people,
   How I had mov'd them. Bring me to Octavius.

                                [*Exeunt.*]

Scene 3. *Rome. A street.*

Enter Cinna the Poet, and after him the Plebeians.

Cinna. I dreamt to-night that I did feast with
   Caesar,
   And things unluckily charge my fantasy.[178]
   I have no will to wander forth[179] of doors,
   Yet something leads me forth.

1 Plebeian. What is your name?   5

2 Plebeian. Whither are you going?

3 Plebeian. Where do you dwell?

4 Plebeian. Are you a married man or a bachelor?

2 Plebeian. Answer every man directly.

---

[173] *straight*: go straightaway.
[174] *upon a wish*: just as I wished.
[175] *Are rid*: have ridden (their horses).
[176] *Belike*: most likely.
[177] *notice*: news.
[178] *charge my fantasy*: influence my dreams, imaginings.
[179] *forth*: out.

1 Plebeian. Ay, and briefly.   10

4 Plebeian. Ay, and wisely.

3 Plebeian. Ay, and truly, you were best.[180]

Cinna. What is my name? Whither am I going?
    Where do I dwell? Am I a married man or a
    bachelor? Then to answer every man directly
    and briefly, wisely and truly: wisely, I say I am a   15
    bachelor.

2 Plebeian. That's as much as to say they are
    fools that marry. You'll bear me a bang[181] for that, I
    fear. Proceed directly.

Cinna. Directly, I am going to Caesar's funeral.   20

1 Plebeian. As a friend or an enemy?

Cinna. As a friend.

2 Plebeian. That matter is answered directly.

4 Plebeian. For your dwelling—briefly.

Cinna. Briefly, I dwell by the Capitol.   25

3 Plebeian. Your name, sir, truly.

Cinna. Truly, my name is Cinna.

1 Plebeian. Tear him to pieces; he's a
    conspirator!

Cinna. I am Cinna the poet, I am Cinna the poet.

4 Plebeian. Tear him for his bad verses, tear him   30
    for his bad verses!

---

[180] *you were best*: it would be best for you.
[181] *You'll bear me a bang*: (1) you will deserve a blow from me; (2) you will
endure a blow from me.

Cinna. I am not Cinna the conspirator.

4 *Plebeian.* It is no matter, his name's Cinna;
    pluck but his name out of his heart, and turn
    him going.[182]

3 *Plebeian.* Tear him, tear him! Come, brands,   35
    ho! fire-brands! To Brutus', to Cassius'! Burn
    all! Some to Decius' house, and some to Casca's;
    some to Ligarius'. Away, go!

                    [*Exeunt all the Plebeians with Cinna.*]

---

[182] *turn him going*: dispatch, kill him.

ACT 4

Scene 1. *Rome. Antony's house.*

Enter Antony, Octavius, and Lepidus.

Antony. These many, then, shall die; their names
   are prick'd.[1]

Octavius. Your brother[2] too must die. Consent
   you, Lepidus?

Lepidus. I do consent.

Octavius.   Prick him down, Antony.

Lepidus. Upon condition Publius shall not live,
   Who is your sister's son, Mark Antony.   5

Antony. He shall not live; look, with a spot I
   damn him.[3]
   But, Lepidus, go you to Caesar's house;
   Fetch the will hither, and we shall determine
   How to cut off some charge in legacies.[4]

Lepidus. What, shall I find you here?   10

Octavius. Or[5] here or at the Capitol.

                                        [*Exit Lepidus.*]

Antony. This is a slight unmeritable[6] man,
   Meet to be sent on errands. Is it fit,

---

[1] *prick'd*: marked off on a list.

[2] *brother*: Lucius Aemilius Paulus (d. 216 B.C.), onetime consul.

[3] *with a spot I damn him*: with a mark (on the wax tablet) I doom him to death.

[4] *cut off some charge in legacies*: I.e., they are proposing to reduce Caesar's bequests to reduce costs.

[5] *Or*: either.

[6] *slight unmeritable*: insignificant undeserving.

91

The threefold world divided,[7] he should stand
One of the three to share it?

Octavius. So you thought him, 15
And took his voice[8] who should be prick'd to die
In our black sentence[9] and proscription.[10]

Antony. Octavius, I have seen more days than
you;[11]
And though we lay these honours on this man,
To ease ourselves of divers sland'rous loads,[12] 20
He shall but bear them as the <u>ass</u> bears gold,
The groan and sweat under the business,[13]
Either led or driven as we point the way;
And having brought our treasure where we will,
Then take we down his load, and turn him off,[14] 25
Like to the empty[15] <u>ass,</u> to shake his ears[16]
And graze in commons.[17]

Octavius. You may do your will;
But he's a tried and valiant soldier.

Antony. So is my horse, Octavius, and for that
I do appoint[18] him store of provender.[19] 30
It is a creature that I teach to fight,
To wind,[20] to stop, to run directly on,

---

[7] *threefold world divided*: The empire was classically divided into Asia, Europe, and Africa (later divided into three parts with the triumvirate).

[8] *took his voice*: accepted his suggestion.

[9] *black sentence*: sentence of death.

[10] *proscription*: outlawry.

[11] *I have seen more days than you*: I am older than you.

[12] *divers sland'rous loads*: a host of accusations and blame cast on various people.

[13] *business*: labor, hard work.

[14] *turn him off*: shoo him away.

[15] *empty*: unburdened, cleared off.

[16] *shake his ears*: a dismissive gesture (also used as a common dismissive insult).

[17] *graze in commons*: go and graze among the common lands.

[18] *appoint*: grant, allot.

[19] *provender*: food.

[20] *wind*: wheel around, turn rapidly (horse riding term).

His corporal[21] motion govern'd by my spirit.[22]
And, in some taste,[23] is Lepidus but so:[24]
He must be taught, and train'd, and bid go forth;   35
A barren-spirited[25] fellow; one that feeds
On objects, arts, and imitations,[26]
Which, out of use and stal'd[27] by other men,
Begin his fashion.[28] Do not talk of him
But as a property.[29] And now, Octavius,   40
Listen great things: Brutus and Cassius
Are levying powers;[30] we must straight[31] make
     head;[32]
Therefore let our alliance be combin'd,
Our best friends made,[33] our means stretch'd;[34]
And let us presently[35] go sit in council   45
How covert matters may be best disclos'd,
And open perils surest answered.[36]

Octavius. Let us do so; for we are at the stake,
     And bay'd about with many enemies;[37]

---

[21] *corporal*: physical.

[22] *spirit*: mind.

[23] *taste*: ways.

[24] *so*: the same.

[25] *barren-spirited*: lacking spirit or initiative.

[26] *objects, arts, and imitations*: strange things, artifices, and fashionable ideas (rather than reality).

[27] *stal'd*: made common by overuse.

[28] *Begin his fashion*: are mistakenly taken by him as the latest fashion.

[29] *property*: prop, tool.

[30] *powers*: armies.

[31] *straight*: straightaway, immediately.

[32] *make head*: gather or advance.

[33] *best friends made*: closest allies chosen.

[34] *stretch'd*: made the most of, extended to the greatest advantage.

[35] *presently*: at once, immediately.

[36] *answered*: dealt with.

[37] *at the stake . . . with many enemies*: caught and toyed with by many enemies (a metaphor taken from the popular sport of bearbaiting, where the animal was tied to a stake and tormented).

And some that smile have in their hearts, I fear, 50
Millions of mischiefs.[38]   [*Exeunt.*]

Scene 2. *The Camp near Sardis. Before the tent of Brutus.*

*Drum. Enter Brutus, Lucilius, Lucius, and the Army.
Titinius and Pindarus meet them.*

Brutus. Stand, ho!

Lucilius. Give the word,[39] ho! and stand.

Brutus. What now, Lucilius? Is Cassius near?

Lucilius. He is at hand, and Pindarus is come
To do you salutation from his master.   5

Brutus. He greets me well.[40] Your master,
 Pindarus,
In his own change,[41] or by ill officers,[42]
Hath given me some worthy[43] cause to wish
Things done undone; but if he be at hand
I shall be satisfied.[44]

Pindarus.   I do not doubt   10
But that my noble master will appear
Such as he is, full of regard[45] and honour.

Brutus. He is not doubted. A word, Lucilius,
How he receiv'd you; let me be resolv'd.[46]

[38] *mischiefs*: plans to do harm (to Octavius and Antony).
[39] *Give the word*: pass down the command, pass on the order.
[40] *greets me well*: sends me greetings by a worthy messenger.
[41] *In his own change*: through a change in his own feelings. Some versions read "charge" instead of "change".
[42] *ill officers*: disloyal advisors.
[43] *worthy*: worthwhile, considerable.
[44] *satisfied*: i.e., with an explanation.
[45] *full of regard*: worthy of reverence, regard.
[46] *let me be resolv'd*: let it be explained to me.

Lucilius. With courtesy and with respect
    enough,   *15*
  But not with such familiar instances[47]
  Nor with such free and friendly conference[48]
  As he hath us'd of old.

Brutus.   w/ Cassius   Thou hast describ'd
  A hot friend cooling. Ever note, Lucilius,
  When love begins to sicken and decay,   *20*
  It useth an enforced ceremony.[49]
  There are no tricks in plain and simple faith;
  But hollow[50] men, like horses hot at hand,[51]
  Make gallant show and promise of their mettle;[52]
  But when they should endure the bloody spur,   *25*
  They fall their crests,[53] and like deceitful jades[54]
  Sink in the trial.[55] Comes his army on?

Lucilius. They mean this night in Sardis to be
    quarter'd.
  The greater part, the horse in general,[56]
  Are come with Cassius.   [*Low march within.*]

Brutus.   Hark! he is arriv'd: *30*
  March gently[57] on to meet him.

Enter Cassius and his Powers.

Cassius. Stand, ho!

Brutus. Stand, ho! Speak the word along.

---

[47] *familiar instances*: marks or demonstrations of friendship.
[48] *conference*: conversation, interaction.
[49] *enforced ceremony*: awkward, strained formality.
[50] *hollow*: insincere, false.
[51] *hot at hand*: too eager from the start (a metaphor taken from horse riding).
[52] *mettle*: strength, worth.
[53] *fall their crests*: let down their heads (the crest is the ridge of a horse's neck).
[54] *jades*: (1) useless horses; (2) nagging women.
[55] *Sink in the trial*: fail when tested.
[56] *horse in general*: main cavalry.
[57] *gently*: slowly, cautiously.

1 Soldier. Stand!

2 Soldier. Stand!   35

3 Soldier. Stand!

Cassius. Most noble brother, you have done me
    wrong.

Brutus. Judge me, you gods! wrong I mine
    enemies?
    And, if not so, how should I wrong a brother?

Cassius. Brutus, this sober form[58] of yours hides
    wrongs;   40
    And when you do them—

Brutus.   Cassius, be content;[59]
    Speak your griefs[60] softly; I do know you well.
    Before the eyes of both our armies here,
    Which should perceive nothing but love from
      us,
    Let us not wrangle. Bid them move away;   45
    Then in my tent, Cassius, enlarge[61] your griefs,
    And I will give you audience.

Cassius.   Pindarus,
    Bid our commanders lead their charges[62] off
    A little from this ground.

Brutus. Lucilius, do you the like; and let no man   50
    Come to our tent till we have done our
      conference.
    Let Lucius and Titinius guard our door.

                      [Exeunt.]

---

[58] *form*: manner.
[59] *content*: calm.
[60] *griefs*: grievances.
[61] *enlarge*: expand upon, express freely.
[62] *charges*: troops.

Scene 3. *The Camp near Sardis. Within the tent of Brutus.*

Enter Brutus and Cassius.

Cassius. That you have wrong'd me doth appear
    in this:
    You have condemn'd and noted[63] Lucius Pella
    For taking bribes here of the Sardians;
    Wherein my letters, praying on his side,
    Because I knew the man, were slighted off.[64]   5

Brutus. You wrong'd yourself to write in such a
    case.

Cassius. In such a time as this it is not meet
    That every nice[65] offence should bear his
    comment.[66]

Brutus. Let me tell you, Cassius, you yourself
    Are much condemn'd to have[67] an itching palm,[68]   10
    To sell and mart[69] your offices for gold
    To undeservers.

Cassius.   I an itching palm!
    You know that you are Brutus that speaks this,
    Or, by the gods, this speech were else your last.

Brutus. The name of Cassius honours[70] this
    corruption,   15
    And chastisement doth therefore hide his head.

Cassius. Chastisement!

---

[63] *noted:* disgraced publicly.

[64] *slighted off:* dismissed, ignored.

[65] *nice:* trivial, unimportant.

[66] *his comment:* criticism.

[67] *condemn'd to have:* reported to have, blamed for having.

[68] *an itching palm:* I.e., he is mercenary, eager for money.

[69] *mart:* traffic in.

[70] *honours:* dignifies, gives an air of respectability to.

Brutus. Remember March, the ides of March
      remember:
   Did not great Julius bleed for justice sake?
   What villian touch'd his body, that did stab,   20
   And not for[71] justice? What, shall one of us,
   That struck the foremost man of all this world
   But for supporting robbers,[72] shall we now
   Contaminate our fingers with base bribes,
   And sell the mighty space of our large honours[73]   25
   For so much trash[74] as may be grasped thus?
   I had rather be a dog and bay[75] the moon
   Than such a Roman.

Cassius.   Brutus, bait[76] not me!
   I'll not endure it. You forget yourself,
   To hedge me in.[77] I am a soldier, I,   30
   Older in practice, abler than yourself
   To make conditions.[78]

Brutus.   Go to; you are not, Cassius.

Cassius. I am.

Brutus. I say you are not.

Cassius. Urge[79] me no more, I shall forget myself;   35
   Have mind upon your health, tempt[80] me no
      farther.

---

[71] *And not for*: except for.

[72] *robbers*: dishonest men, officials.

[73] *mighty space of our large honours*: our capacity for being magnanimous and generous.

[74] *trash*: i.e., money.

[75] *bay*: bark or howl at.

[76] *bait*: provoke.

[77] *hedge me in*: impose limits on me.

[78] *make conditions*: handle matters, deal with a situation.

[79] *Urge*: bully, harass.

[80] *tempt*: i.e., provoke to violence.

Brutus. Away, slight[81] man!

Cassius. Is't possible?

Brutus.   Hear me, for I will speak.
  Must I give way and room to your rash choler?[82]
  Shall I be frighted when a madman stares?   40

Cassius. O ye gods, ye gods! must I endure all
    this?

Brutus. All this? Ay, more! Fret till your proud
    heart break.
  Go show your slaves how choleric you are,
  And make your bondmen tremble. Must I
    budge?
  Must I observe[83] you? Must I stand and crouch[84]   45
  Under your testy[85] humour? By the gods,
  You shall digest the venom of your spleen[86]
  Though it do split you; for from this day forth
  I'll use you for my mirth, yea, for my laughter,
  When you are waspish.

Cassius.   Is it come to this?   50

Brutus. You say you are a better soldier.
  Let it appear so; make your vaunting[87] true,
  And it shall please me well. For mine own part,
  I shall be glad to learn of[88] noble men.

---

[81] *slight*: unimportant, insignificant.

[82] *choler*: anger. The term is taken from a theory originating with Greek physicians, including Hippocrates (469–399 B.C.), which argued that human temperaments were derived from four bodily humors, including yellow bile (the source of the choleric temperament).

[83] *observe*: wait on.

[84] *crouch*: bow.

[85] *testy*: irritable.

[86] *spleen*: temper (the spleen was considered the bodily source of sudden passions).

[87] *vaunting*: boasting, claims.

[88] *of*: (1) about; (2) from.

Cassius. You wrong me every way; you wrong
    me, Brutus;   55
  I said an elder soldier, not a better.
  Did I say 'better'?

Brutus.   If you did, I care not.

Cassius. When Caesar liv'd, he durst not thus
  have mov'd[89] me.

Brutus. Peace, peace! You durst not so have
  tempted[90] him.

Cassius. I durst not?   60

Brutus. No.

Cassius. What, durst not tempt him?

Brutus.   For your life you durst not.

Cassius. Do not presume too much upon my love;
  I may do that I shall be sorry for.

Brutus. You have done that you should be sorry
    for.   65
  There is no terror, Cassius, in your threats;
  For I am arm'd so strong in honesty
  That they[91] pass by me as the idle wind,
  Which I respect not.[92] I did send to you
  For certain sums of gold, which you denied me;   70
  For I can raise no money by vile means.
  By heaven, I had rather coin my heart,
  And drop my blood for drachmas, than to wring
  From the hard hands of peasants their vile trash
  By any indirection.[93] I did send   75
  To you for gold to pay my legions,

---

[89] *mov'd*: roused, infuriated.
[90] *tempted*: provoked.
[91] *they*: i.e., his threats.
[92] *respect not*: ignore, heed not at all.
[93] *indirection*: crooked or roundabout means.

Which you denied me; was that done like
    Cassius?
Should I have answer'd Caius Cassius so?
When Marcus Brutus grows so covetous,
To lock such rascal counters[94] from his friends,   80
Be ready, gods, with all your thunderbolts,
Dash him to pieces!

Cassius.   I denied you not.

Brutus. You did.

Cassius.   I did not. He was but a fool
  That brought my answer back.
  Brutus hath riv'd[95] my heart.
  A friend should bear his friend's infirmities,   85
  But Brutus makes mine greater than they are.

Brutus. I do not, till you practise them on me.

Cassius. You love me not.

Brutus.   I do not like your faults.

Cassius. A friendly eye could never see such
    faults.

Brutus. A flatterer's would not, though they do
    appear   90
  As huge as high Olympus.

Cassius. Come, Antony, and young Octavius,
    come,
  Revenge yourselves alone on Cassius,
  For Cassius is aweary of the world:
  Hated by one he loves; brav'd[96] by his brother;   95
  Check'd[97] like a bondman; all his faults observ'd,

---

[94] *rascal counters*: base coinage (i.e., the "vile trash" he mentions above).
[95] *riv'd*: broken, torn apart.
[96] *brav'd*: defied.
[97] *Check'd*: rebuked.

Set in a notebook, learn'd, and conn'd by rote,[98]
To cast into my teeth. O, I could weep
My spirit from mine eyes! There is my dagger,
And here my naked breast; within, a heart   100
Dearer than Pluto's mine,[99] richer than gold;
If that thou be'st a Roman, take it forth.
I, that[100] denied thee gold, will give my heart.
Strike as thou didst at Caesar; for I know,
When thou didst hate him worst, thou lov'dst
   him better   105
Than ever thou lov'dst Cassius.

Brutus.   Sheathe your dagger.
  Be angry when you will, it shall have scope;[101]
  Do what you will, dishonour shall be humour.[102]
  O Cassius, you are yoked with a lamb,
  That carries anger as the flint bears fire;   110
  Who, much enforced,[103] shows a hasty spark,
  And straight is cold again.

Cassius.   Hath Cassius liv'd
  To be but mirth and laughter to his Brutus,
  When grief and blood ill-temper'd[104] vexeth him?

Brutus. When I spoke that I was ill-temper'd too.   115

Cassius. Do you confess so much? Give me your
  hand.

Brutus. And my heart too.

---

[98] *conn'd by rote*: learned by memorization (like an ignorant schoolboy).

[99] *Pluto's mine*: Two gods of classical mythology—Pluto, god of the underworld, and Plutus, the god of riches—are conflated here.

[100] *that*: who.

[101] *scope*: room to work (i.e., in battling their common foes).

[102] *dishonour shall be humour*: (1) even dishonorable deeds will be humored; (2) dishonorable deeds or words shall be dismissed as expressions of a man's humor.

[103] *enforced*: provoked, forced by circumstances.

[104] *blood ill-temper'd*: i.e., dark mood (associated with the theory of the four bodily humors).

Cassius.   O Brutus!

Brutus.   What's the matter?

Cassius. Have not you love enough to bear with me,
   When that rash humour which my mother gave me
   Makes me forgetful?   120

Brutus. Yes, Cassius; and from henceforth,
   When you are over-earnest with your Brutus,
   He'll think your mother chides,[105] and leave you so.

Enter a Poet, followed by Lucilius, Titinius, and Lucius.

Poet. Let me go in to see the generals.
   There is some grudge between 'em; 'tis not meet
   They be alone.

Lucilius. You shall not come to them.   125

Poet. Nothing but death shall stay me.

Cassius. How now! What's the matter?

Poet. For shame, you generals! What do you mean?
   Love, and be friends, as two such men should be;
   For I have seen more years, I'm sure, than ye.   130

Cassius. Ha, ha! How vilely doth this cynic[106]
   rhyme!

Brutus. Get you hence, sirrah;[107] saucy fellow,
   hence!

Cassius. Bear with him, Brutus: 'tis his fashion.

---

[105] *He'll think your mother chides*: I.e., Brutus will think that the moody nature
with which Cassius was born is prompting him to speak in this way.
   [106] *cynic*: rude fellow.
   [107] *sirrah*: term of address to inferiors.

Brutus. I'll know his humour when he knows his
  time.[108]
 What should the wars do with these jigging[109]
  fools?   *135*
 Companion,[110] hence!

Cassius.   Away, away, be gone!

             [*Exit Poet.*]

Brutus. Lucilius and Titinius, bid the
  commanders
 Prepare to lodge their companies to-night.

Cassius. And come yourselves, and bring
  Messala with you
 Immediately to us.

      [*Exeunt Lucilius and Titinius.*]

Brutus.   Lucius, a bowl of wine! *140*

            [*Exit Lucius.*]

Cassius. I did not think you could have been so
  angry.

Brutus. O Cassius, I am sick of many griefs!

Cassius. Of your philosophy you make no use,
 If you give place to[111] accidental evils.

Brutus. No man bears sorrow better. Portia is
  dead.   *145*

Cassius. Ha! Portia?

Brutus. She is dead.

---

 [108] *I'll know his humour when he knows his time*: I will accept his eccentric
humor when he is a better judge of when it is appropriate.
 [109] *jigging*: (1) rhyming; (2) frivolous.
 [110] *Companion*: rude fellow.
 [111] *give place to*: give in to, submit to.

Cassius. How scap'd I killing when I cross'd you
     so?
   O insupportable and touching loss!
   Upon what sickness?

Brutus.   Impatient of[112] my absence,   *150*
   And grief that young Octavius with Mark
     Antony
   Have made themselves so strong; for with her
     death
   That tidings[113] came. With this she fell distract,[114]
   And, her attendants absent, swallow'd fire.[115]

Cassius. And died so?

Brutus. Even so.

Cassius. O ye immortal gods!   *155*

Enter Lucius with wine and tapers.

Brutus. Speak no more of her. Give me a bowl of
     wine.
   In this I bury all unkindness, Cassius.   [*Drinks.*]

Cassius. My heart is thirsty for that noble pledge.
   Fill, Lucius, till the wine o'erswell the cup;
   I cannot drink too much of Brutus' love.   *160*

                [*Drinks. Exit Lucius.*]

Re-enter Titinius, with Messala.

Brutus. Come in, Titinius! Welcome, good
     Messala!

---

[112] *Impatient of*: unable to endure.

[113] *tidings*: i.e., the news (of the strength of Antony and Octavius).

[114] *distract*: distraught.

[115] *And, her attendants absent, swallow'd fire*: According to Plutarch, Portia killed herself by choking on hot coals.

Now sit we close about this taper here,
And call in question[116] our necessities.

Cassius. Portia, art thou gone?

Brutus.   No more, I pray you.
Messala, I have here received letters,   165
That young Octavius and Mark Antony
Come down upon us with a mighty power,[117]
Bending their expedition toward Philippi.

Messala. Myself have letters of the self-same
     tenour.

Brutus. With what addition?   170

Messala. That, by proscription and bills of
     outlawry,[118]
Octavius, Antony, and Lepidus
Have put to death an hundred senators.

Brutus. Therein our letters do not well agree;
Mine speak of seventy senators that died   175
By their proscriptions, Cicero being one.

Cassius. Cicero one!

Messala.   Cicero is dead,
And by that order of proscription.
Had you your letters from your wife, my lord?

Brutus. No, Messala.

Messala. Nor nothing in your letters writ of her?   180

Brutus. Nothing, Messala.

Messala.   That, methinks is strange.

---

[116] *call in question*: discuss.

[117] *power*: armed force.

[118] *proscription and bills of outlawry*: condemnations to death and lists of the names of those condemned.

Brutus. Why ask you? Hear you aught of her in
    yours?

Messala. No, my lord.

Brutus. Now, as you are a Roman, tell me true.   185

Messala. Then like a Roman bear the truth I tell:
    For certain she is dead, and by strange manner.

Brutus. Why, farewell, Portia. We must die,
    Messala.
    With meditating that she must die once,
    I have the patience to endure it now.   190

Messala. Even so great men great losses should
    endure.

Cassius. I have as much of this[119] in art[120] as you,
    But yet my nature could not bear it so.

Brutus. Well, to our work alive. What do you
    think
    Of marching to Philippi presently?   195

Cassius. I do not think it good.

Brutus.   Your reason?

Cassius.   This it is:
    'Tis better that the enemy seek us;
    So shall he waste his means, weary his soldiers,
    Doing himself offence,[121] whilst we, lying still,
    Are full of rest, defence, and nimbleness.   200

Brutus. Good reasons must, of force,[122] give place to better.
    The people 'twixt Philippi and this ground

[119] *this:* i.e., Stoicism, a school of philosophy built upon the absolute control and repression of emotions.
[120] *art:* theory.
[121] *offence:* harm.
[122] *force:* necessity.

Do stand but in a forc'd affection;[123]
For they have grudg'd us contribution.
The enemy, marching along by them,   205
By them shall make a fuller number up,
Come on refresh'd, new-added,[124] and encourag'd;
From which advantage shall we cut him off,
If at Philippi we do face him there,
These people at our back.

Cassius.   Hear me, good brother. 210

Brutus. Under your pardon. You must note
  beside
That we have tried the utmost of our friends,
Our legions are brim full, our cause is ripe.
The enemy increaseth every day:
We, at the height, are ready to decline. 215
There is a tide in the affairs of men
Which, taken at the flood, leads on to fortune;
Omitted, all the voyage of their life
Is bound in shallows and in miseries.
On such a full sea are we now afloat, 220
And we must take the current when it serves,
Or lose our ventures.[125]

Cassius.   Then, with your will, go on;
We'll along[126] ourselves and meet them at Philippi.

Brutus. The deep of night is crept upon our talk, 225
And nature must obey necessity,
Which we will niggard[127] with a little rest.
There is no more to say?

---

[123] *The people . . . stand but in a forc'd affection*: I.e., the people are not spontaneously loyal but have been forced to be loyal by fear of the rebel forces.
[124] *new-added*: reinforced.
[125] *ventures*: i.e., all that has been risked thus far.
[126] *along*: go along.
[127] *niggard*: treat in a miserly manner (i.e., nature demands sleep, but they will satisfy it only with the bare minimum of rest).

Cassius.   No more. Good night:
  Early to-morrow will we rise, and hence.

Brutus. Lucius! [*Enter Lucius.*] My gown.[128]   230
  [*Exit Lucius.*] Farewell, good Messala.
  Good night, Titinius. Noble, noble Cassius,
  Good night, and good repose!

Cassius.   O my dear brother,
  This was an ill beginning of the night!
  Never come[129] such division 'tween our souls!
  Let it not, Brutus.

Brutus.   Everything is well.

Cassius. Good night, my lord.   235

Brutus.   Good night, good brother.

Titinius and Messala. Good night, Lord
      Brutus.

Brutus. Farewell, every one.

                  [*Exeunt Cassius, Titinius, and Messala.*]

Re-enter Lucius with the gown.

  Give me the gown. Where is thy instrument?[130]

Lucius. Here in the tent.

Brutus.   What, thou speak'st drowsily?
  Poor knave,[131] I blame thee not; thou art
      o'erwatch'd.[132]
  Call Claudius and some other of my men;   240
  I'll have them sleep on cushions in my tent.

---

[128] *gown*: dressing gown.
[129] *Never come*: may there never again come.
[130] *instrument*: probably a lute (a stringed instrument).
[131] *knave*: lad (not necessarily used angrily).
[132] *o'erwatch'd*: tired from lack of sleep.

Lucius. Varro and Claudius!

Enter Varro and Claudius.

Varro. Calls my lord?

Brutus. I pray you, sirs, lie in my tent and sleep;
  It may be I shall raise you by and by   245
  On business[133] to my brother Cassius.

Varro. So please you we will stand and watch
    your pleasure.[134]

Brutus. I will not have it so. Lie down, good sirs;
  It may be I shall otherwise bethink me.[135]
  Look, Lucius, here's the book I sought for so;   250
  I put it in the pocket of my gown.

                  [*Varro and Claudius lie down.*]

Lucius. I was sure your lordship did not give it
    me.

Brutus. Bear with me, good boy, I am much
    forgetful.
  Canst thou hold up thy heavy eyes awhile,
  And touch[136] thy instrument a strain or two?   255

Lucius. Ay,[137] my lord, an't[138] please you.

Brutus.   It does, my boy.
  I trouble thee too much, but thou art willing.

Lucius. It is my duty, sir.

---

[133] *raise you by and by/On business*: awaken you and send you on business.
[134] *watch your pleasure*: stay awake in case you desire us to do something.
[135] *otherwise bethink me*: change my mind.
[136] *touch*: play.
[137] *Ay*: yes.
[138] *an't*: if it.

Brutus. I should not urge thy duty past thy
    might;
I know young bloods[139] look for a time of rest.   260

Lucius. I have slept, my lord, already.

Brutus. It was well done; and thou shall sleep
    again;
I will not hold thee long. If I do live,
I will be good to thee.

        [*Music and a song. Lucius falls asleep.*]

This is a sleepy tune. O murd'rous[140] slumber!   265
Layest thou thy leaden mace[141] upon my boy,
That plays thee music? Gentle knave, good
    night.
I will not do thee so much wrong to wake thee.
If thou dost nod, thou break'st thy instrument;
I'll take it from thee; and, good boy, good
    night.   270
Let me see, let me see; is not the leaf turn'd
    down
Where I left reading? Here it is, I think.

        [*Sits down.*]

Enter the Ghost of Caesar.

How ill this taper burns! Ha! who comes here?
I think it is the weakness of mine eyes
That shapes this monstrous[142] apparition.   275
It comes upon me. Art thou any thing?
Art thou some god, some angel, or some devil,

[139] *young bloods*: constitutions of young men.
[140] *murd'rous*: deathlike.
[141] *leaden mace*: heavy rod of authority (like that used by bailiffs making an arrest).
[142] *monstrous*: horrifying but also wondrous.

That mak'st my blood cold and my hair to
    stare?[143]
Speak to me what thou art.

Ghost. Thy evil spirit, Brutus.

Brutus.   Why com'st thou?   280

Ghost. To tell thee thou shalt see me at Philippi.

Brutus. Well; then I shall see thee again?

Ghost. Ay, at Philippi.

Brutus. Why, I will see thee at Philippi, then.

                              [*Exit Ghost.*]

Now I have taken heart thou vanishest.   285
Ill spirit, I would hold more talk with thee.
Boy! Lucius! Varro! Claudius! Sirs, awake!
Claudius!

Lucius. The strings, my lord, are false.[144]

Brutus. He thinks he still is at his instrument.   290
    Lucius, awake!

Lucius. My lord!

Brutus. Didst thou dream, Lucius, that thou so
    criedst out?

Lucius. My lord, I do not know that I did cry.

Brutus. Yes, that thou didst. Didst thou see any
    thing?   295

Lucius. Nothing, my lord.

---

[143] *stare*: stand on end.
[144] *false*: out of tune.

Brutus. Sleep again, Lucius. Sirrah Claudius!
   [*To Varro*] Fellow thou, awake!

Varro. My lord?

Claudius. My lord?   300

Brutus. Why did you so cry out, sirs, in your
   sleep?

Both. Did we, my lord?

Brutus.   Ay. Saw you any thing?

Varro. No, my lord, I saw nothing.

Claudius.   Nor I, my lord.

Brutus. Go and commend me to my brother
   Cassius;
   Bid him set on his pow'rs betimes[145] before,   305
   And we will follow.

Varro and Claudius. It shall be done, my lord.

                       [*Exeunt.*]

---

[145] *betimes*: early in the morning.

ACT 5

Scene 1. *Near Philippi.*

Enter Octavius, Antony, and their Army.

Octavius. Now, Antony, our hopes are
    answered.
  You said the enemy would not come down,
  But keep the hills and upper regions;
  It proves not so. Their battles[1] are at hand;
  They mean to warn[2] us at Philippi here,   5
  Answering before we do demand of them.[3]

Antony. Tut, I am in their bosoms,[4] and I know
  Wherefore they do it. They could be content
  To visit other places, and come down
  With fearful bravery,[5] thinking by this face   10
  To fasten in our thoughts that they have
    courage;
  But 'tis not so.

Enter a Messenger.

Messenger.   Prepare you, generals:
  The enemy comes on in gallant show;
  Their bloody sign of battle[6] is hung out,
  And something to be done immediately.   15

Antony. Octavius, lead your battle softly[7] on,
  Upon the left hand of the even field.

---

  [1] *battles*: armies, forces.
  [2] *warn*: attack, challenge, face.
  [3] *Answering before we do demand of them*: preparing for battle before receiving a challenge from us.
  [4] *I am in their bosoms*: I can read their plans and thoughts.
  [5] *fearful bravery*: intimidating ferocity (or bravado).
  [6] *bloody sign of battle*: red flag.
  [7] *softly*: carefully, cautiously, warily.

114

Octavius. Upon the right hand I: keep thou the
    left.

Antony. Why do you cross[8] me in this exigent?[9]

Octavius. I do not cross you; but I will do so.   20

                        [*March.*]

*Drum. Enter Brutus, Cassius, and their Army;
Lucilius, Titinius, Messala, and Others.*

Brutus. They stand, and would have parley.[10]

Cassius. Stand fast, Titinius; we must out and
    talk.

Octavius. Mark Antony, shall we give sign of
    battle?

Antony. No, Caesar, we will answer on their
    charge.[11]
  Make forth;[12] the generals would have some
  words.   25

Octavius. Stir not until the signal.

Brutus. Words before blows. Is it so,
    countrymen?

Octavius. Not that we love words better, as you
    do.

Brutus. Good words are better than bad strokes,
    Octavius.

---

[8] *cross:* contradict, oppose.
[9] *exigent:* moment of crisis.
[10] *parley:* negotiating conversation.
[11] *answer on their charge:* counter them when they attack.
[12] *Make forth:* move forward.

Antony. In your bad strokes, Brutus, you give
    good words;   30
  Witness the hole you made in Caesar's heart,
  Crying 'Long live! Hail, Caesar!'

Cassius.   Antony,
  The posture[13] of your blows are[14] yet unknown;
  But for your words, they rob the Hybla[15] bees,
  And leave them honeyless.

Antony.   Not stingless too?   35

Brutus. O yes, and soundless too;
  For you have stol'n their buzzing, Antony,
  And very wisely threat before you sting.

Antony. Villains, you did not so when your vile
    daggers
  Hack'd one another in the sides of Caesar.   40
  You show'd your teeth[16] like apes, and fawn'd like
    hounds,
  And bow'd like bondmen, kissing Caesar's feet;
  Whilst damned Casca, like a cur, behind
  Struck Caesar on the neck. O you flatterers!

Cassius. Flatterers! Now, Brutus, thank yourself: 45
  This tongue had not offended so to-day
  If Cassius might have rul'd.[17]

Octavius. Come, come, the cause. If arguing
    make us sweat,
  The proof of it[18] will turn to redder drops.

---

[13] *posture*: quality.
[14] *are*: is.
[15] *Hybla*: town in Sicily renowned for the quality of its honey.
[16] *show'd your teeth*: smiled menacingly.
[17] *This tongue . . . might have rul'd*: Cassius wanted to kill Antony immediately after the death of Caesar.
[18] *proof of it*: i.e., fighting.

Look,   50
I draw a sword against conspirators;
When think you that the sword goes up[19] again?
Never till Caesar's three and thirty wounds
Be well aveng'd, or till another Caesar
Have added slaughter[20] to the sword of traitors.   55

Brutus. Caesar, thou canst not die by traitors'
    hands,
Unless thou bring'st them with thee.

Octavius.   So I hope.
I was not born to die on Brutus' sword.

Brutus. O, if thou wert the noblest of thy strain,[21]
    Young man, thou couldst not die more
      honourable.   60

Cassius. A peevish[22] schoolboy, worthless of such honour,
    Join'd with a masker and a reveller![23]

Antony. Old Cassius still!

Octavius.   Come, Antony; away!
Defiance, traitors, hurl we in your teeth.
If you dare fight to-day, come to the field;   65
If not, when you have stomachs.[24]

      [*Exeunt Octavius, Antony, and their Army.*]

Cassius. Why, now, blow wind, swell billow, and
    swim bark!
The storm is up, and all is on the hazard.[25]

Brutus. Ho, Lucilius! hark, a word with you.

---

[19] *goes up*: is sheathed.
[20] *till another Caesar / Have added slaughter*: i.e., until Octavius is himself killed.
[21] *strain*: family, bloodline.
[22] *peevish*: silly, childish.
[23] *a masker and a reveller*: i.e., Antony.
[24] *stomachs*: i.e., appetites for battle.
[25] *on the hazard*: at stake, gambled.

Lucilius. My lord.

[*Brutus and Lucilius converse apart.*]

Cassius. Messala.

Messala.   What says my general?

Cassius.   Messala,   70
    This is my birth-day; as this very day
    Was Cassius born. Give me thy hand, Messala.
    Be thou my witness that against my will,
    As Pompey was,[26] am I compell'd to set
    Upon one battle all our liberties.   75
    You know that I held Epicurus[27] strong,
    And his opinion; now I change my mind,
    And partly credit[28] things that do presage.[29]
    Coming from Sardis, on our former ensign[30]
    Two mighty eagles fell;[31] and there they perch'd,   80
    Gorging and feeding from our soldiers' hands,
    Who[32] to Philippi here consorted[33] us.
    This morning are they fled away and gone,
    And in their steads do ravens, crows, and kites,[34]
    Fly o'er our heads and downward look on us   85
    As we were sickly prey. Their shadows seem
    A canopy most fatal, under which
    Our army lies, ready to give up the ghost.[35]

[26] *As Pompey was*: Pompey was persuaded (against his judgment) to fight at Pharsalus in Thessaly in 48 B.C. and was thoroughly defeated.

[27] *Epicurus*: materialist philosopher (341–270 B.C.) who believed that the gods were indifferent to the actions and fates of men (and who therefore did not believe in omens).

[28] *credit*: believe.

[29] *things that do presage*: omens.

[30] *former ensign*: foremost standards.

[31] *fell*: swooped.

[32] *Who*: which.

[33] *consorted*: accompanied

[34] *ravens, crows, and kites*: birds of prey and ill omen.

[35] *give up the ghost*: die.

Messala. Believe not so.

Cassius.   I but believe it partly;
   For I am fresh of spirit and resolv'd   90
   To meet all perils very constantly.

Brutus. Even so, Lucilius.

Cassius.   Now, most noble Brutus,
   The gods to-day stand friendly, that we may,
   Lovers in peace, lead on our days to age!
   But, since the affairs of men rest still in-certain,[36]   95
   Let's reason with the worst that may befall.[37]
   If we do lose this battle, then is this
   The very last time we shall speak together.
   What are you then determined to do?

Brutus. Even by the rule of that philosophy[38]   100
   By which I did blame Cato for the death
   Which he did give himself—I know not how,
   But I do find it cowardly and vile,
   For fear of what might fall,[39] so to prevent[40]
   The time[41] of life—arming myself with patience   105
   To stay[42] the providence of some high powers
   That govern us below.

Cassius.   Then, if we lose this battle,
   You are contented to be led in triumph[43]
   Thorough the streets of Rome?

---

[36] *rest still in-certain*: must always be in doubt.

[37] *reason with the worst that may befall*: consider the very worst possible outcome.

[38] *that philosophy*: i.e., Stoicism.

[39] *fall*: befall.

[40] *prevent*: (1) forestall; (2) anticipate.

[41] *time*: term, length, extent.

[42] *stay*: await.

[43] *in triumph*: i.e., as a captive.

Brutus. No, Cassius, no. Think not, thou noble
    Roman,   *110*
  That ever Brutus will go bound to Rome;
  He bears too great a mind. But this same day
  Must end that work the ides of March begun,
  And whether we shall meet again I know not.
  Therefore our everlasting farewell take: *115*
  For ever and for ever farewell, Cassius!
  If we do meet again, why, we shall smile;
  If not, why then this parting was well made.

Cassius. For ever and for ever farewell, Brutus!
  If we do meet again, we'll smile indeed;   *120*
  If not, 'tis true this parting was well made.

Brutus. Why then, lead on. O that a man might
    know
  The end of this day's business ere it come!
  But it sufficeth that the day will end,
  And then the end is known. Come, ho! away!   *125*

                             [Exeunt.]

Scene 2. *Near Philippi. The field of battle.*

      Alarum.[44] *Enter Brutus and Messala.*

Brutus. Ride, ride, Messala, ride, and give these
    bills[45]
Unto the legions on the other side.

                          [Loud alarum.]

Let them set on at once; for I perceive
But cold demeanour[46] in Octavius' wing,

[44] *Alarum:* trumpet call to arms.
[45] *bills:* orders.
[46] *cold demeanour:* lack of enthusiasm for the fight.

And sudden push[47] gives them the overthrow.   5
Ride, ride, Messala; let them all come down.[48]

[Exeunt.]

Scene 3. *Another part of the field.*

Alarums. Enter Cassius and Titinius.

Cassius. O, look, Titinius, look, the villains[49] fly!
  Myself have to mine own[50] turn'd enemy.
  This ensign[51] here of mine was turning back;
  I slew the coward, and did take it from him.

Titinius. O Cassius, Brutus gave the word too
    early,   5
  Who, having some advantage on Octavius,
  Took it too eagerly. His soldiers fell to spoil,[52]
  Whilst we by Antony are all enclos'd.

Enter Pindarus.

Pindarus. Fly further off, my lord, fly further off;
  Mark Antony is in your tents, my lord;   10
  Fly, therefore, noble Cassius, fly far[53] off.

Cassius. This hill is far enough. Look, look,
    Titinius.
  Are those my tents where I perceive the fire?

Titinius. They are, my lord.

---

[47] *push*: attack.
[48] *come down*: speed down to the attack.
[49] *villains*: cowards (his own soldiers).
[50] *mine own*: my own soldiers.
[51] *ensign*: standard, flag.
[52] *spoil*: looting bodies.
[53] *far*: farther.

Cassius.   Titinius, if thou lovest me,
    Mount thou my horse and hide thy spurs in
        him,   15
    Till he have brought thee up to yonder troops
    And here again, that I may rest assur'd
    Whether yond troops are friend or enemy.

Titinius. I will be here again even with a
        thought.   [*Exit.*]

Cassius. Go, Pindarus, get higher on that hill;
    My sight was ever thick;⁵⁴ regard Titinius,
    And tell me what thou not'st about the field.   20

                              [*Pindarus goes up.*]

    This day I breathed first. Time is come round,
    And where I did begin there shall I end;
    My life is run his compass.⁵⁵ Sirrah, what news?   25

Pindarus. [*Above*]⁵⁶ O my lord!

Cassius. What news?

Pindarus. Titinius is enclosed round about
    With horsemen that make to him on the spur;⁵⁷
    Yet he spurs on. Now they are almost on him.   30
    Now Titinius! Now some light.⁵⁸ O, he lights too!
    He's ta'en.⁵⁹   [*Shout.*]
    And hark! They shout for joy.

Cassius. Come down; behold no more.
    O, coward that I am to live so long
    To see my best friend ta'en before my face!   35

⁵⁴ *thick*: dim, limited.
⁵⁵ *compass*: allotted length.
⁵⁶ *Above*: i.e., speaking from the upper stage.
⁵⁷ *make to him on the spur*: ride toward him at full speed.
⁵⁸ *light*: alight (from their horses).
⁵⁹ *ta'en*: taken (i.e., made captive).

Enter Pindarus.

> Come hither, sirrah.
> In Parthia did I take thee prisoner;
> And then I swore thee,[60] saving[61] of thy life,
> That whatsoever I did bid thee do
> Thou shouldst attempt it. Come now, keep
>   thine oath;   40
> Now be a freeman, and with this good sword,
> That ran through Caesar's bowels, search[62] this
>   bosom.
> Stand[63] not to answer; here, take thou the hilts;
> And when my face is cover'd, as 'tis now,
> Guide thou the sword. [*Pindarus stabs him.*]
>   Caesar, thou art reveng'd,   45
> Even with the sword that kill'd thee.   [*Dies.*]

Pindarus. So, I am free; yet would not so have
>   been,
> Durst I have done my will. O Cassius!
> Far from this country Pindarus shall run,
> Where never Roman shall take note of him.   50

>   [*Exit.*]

Re-enter Titinius, with Messala.

Messala. It is but change,[64] Titinius; for Octavius
> Is overthrown by noble Brutus' power,
> As Cassius' legions are by Antony.

Titinius. These tidings will well comfort[65] Cassius.

Messala. Where did you leave him?

---

[60] *swore thee*: demanded that you swear.
[61] *saving*: sparing.
[62] *search*: penetrate, probe (i.e., stab).
[63] *Stand*: delay, wait.
[64] *change*: exchange of good fortunes.
[65] *comfort*: give new heart to.

Titinius.   All disconsolate,   55
  With Pindarus, his bondman, on this hill.

Messala. Is not that he that lies upon the
      ground?

Titinius. He lies not like the living. O my heart!

Messala. Is not that he?

Titinius.   No, this was he, Messala;
  But Cassius is no more. O setting sun,   60
  As in thy red rays thou dost sink to night,
  So in his red blood Cassius' day is set!
  The sun of Rome is set. Our day is gone;
  Clouds, dews, and dangers come; our deeds are
      done.
  Mistrust of my success hath done this deed.   65

Messala. Mistrust of good success hath done this
      deed.
  O hateful error, melancholy's child,
  Why dost thou show to the apt[66] thoughts of men
  The things that are not? O error, soon conceiv'd,
  Thou never com'st unto a happy birth,   70
  But kill'st the mother[67] that engend'red[68] thee!

Titinius. What, Pindarus! Where art thou,
      Pindarus?

Messala. Seek him, Titinius, whilst I go to meet
  The noble Brutus, thrusting this report
  Into his ears. I may say 'thrusting' it;   75
  For piercing steel and darts[69] envenomed
  Shall be as welcome to the ears of Brutus
  As tidings of this sight.

[66] *apt*: impressionable.
[67] *mother*: i.e., the melancholy person in whom the error took root.
[68] *engend'red*: conceived.
[69] *darts*: spears or arrows.

Titinius.   Hie you, Messala,
   And I will seek for Pindarus the while.

                           [Exit Messala.]

   Why didst thou send me forth, brave Cassius?   80
   Did I not meet thy friends, and did not they
   Put on my brows this wreath of victory,
   And bid me give it thee? Didst thou not hear
      their shouts?
   Alas, thou hast misconstrued every thing!
   But hold thee, take this garland on thy brow;   85
   Thy Brutus bid me give it thee, and I
   Will do his bidding. Brutus, come apace,
   And see how I regarded Caius Cassius.
   By your leave, gods. This is a Roman's part.
   Come, Cassius' sword, and find Titinius' heart.   90

                              [Dies.]

Alarum. Re-enter Messala, with Brutus, Young Cato,
Strato, Volumnius, and Lucilius.

Brutus. Where, where, Messala, doth his body
   lie?

Messala. Lo yonder, and Titinius mourning it.

Brutus. Titinius' face is upward.

Cato.   He is slain.

Brutus. O Julius Caesar, thou art mighty yet!
   Thy spirit walks abroad and turns our swords   95
   In our own proper[70] entrails.   *[Low alarums.]*

Cato.   Brave Titinius!
   Look whe'r he have not crown'd dead Cassius!

---

[70] *own proper:* very own.

Brutus. Are yet two Romans living such as
    these?
  The last of all the Romans, fare thee well!
  It is impossible that ever Rome   100
  Should breed thy fellow. Friends, I owe moe[71]
    tears
  To this dead man than you shall see me pay.
  I shall find time, Cassius, I shall find time.
  Come, therefore, and to Thasos[72] send his body.
  His funerals shall not be in our camp,   105
  Lest it discomfort[73] us. Lucilius, come;
  And come, young Cato; let us to the field.
  Labeo and Flavius set our battles on.
  'Tis three o'clock; and, Romans, yet ere night
  We shall try fortune in a second fight.   110

                    [*Exeunt.*]

Scene 4. *Another part of the field.*

*Alarum. Enter Brutus, Messala, Young Cato,
Lucilius, and Flavius.*

Brutus. Yet, countrymen, O, yet hold up your
    heads!

Cato. What bastard doth not?[74] Who will go with me?
  I will proclaim my name about the field:
  I am the son of Marcus Cato, ho!
  A foe to tyrants, and my country's friend.   5
  I am the son of Marcus Cato, ho!

Enter Soldiers and fight.

[71] *moe:* more.
[72] *Thasos:* island near Philippi.
[73] *discomfort:* dishearten, discourage.
[74] *What bastard doth not?* Who is so lowborn among us that he would not?

Brutus. And I am Brutus, Marcus Brutus, I!
  Brutus, my country's friend! Know me for
      Brutus!   [*Exit. Young Cato falls.*]

Lucilius. O young and noble Cato, art thou
      down?
  Why, now thou diest as bravely as Titinius,   10
  And mayst be honour'd, being Cato's son.

1 Soldier. Yield, or thou diest.

Lucilius.   Only I yield to die.[75]
  [*Offering money*] There is so much that thou wilt
      kill me straight.
  Kill Brutus, and be honour'd in his death.

1 Soldier. We must not. A noble prisoner!   15

Enter Antony.

2 Soldier. Room, ho! Tell Antony Brutus is ta'en.

1 Soldier. I'll tell the news. Here comes the
      general.
  Brutus is ta'en! Brutus is ta'en, my lord!

Antony. Where is he?

Lucilius. Safe, Antony; Brutus is safe enough.   20
  I dare assure thee that no enemy
  Shall ever take alive the noble Brutus.
  The gods defend him from so great a shame!
  When you do find him, or alive or dead,
  He will be found like Brutus, like himself.[76]   25

Antony. This is not Brutus, friend; but, I assure
      you,
  A prize no less in worth. Keep this man safe;

[75] *Only I yield to die*: I yield only to die.
[76] *like Brutus, like himself*: i.e., behaving as befits so noble a man.

Give him all kindness. I had rather have
Such men my friends than enemies. Go on,
And see whe'r Brutus be alive or dead;   30
And bring us word unto Octavius' tent
How everything is chanc'd.[77]   [*Exeunt.*]

Scene 5. *Another part of the field.*

Enter Brutus, Dardanius, Clitus, Strato, and Volumnius.

Brutus. Come, poor remains[78] of friends, rest on
    this rock.

Clitus. Statilius show'd the torch-light; but, my lord,
    He came not back.[79] He is or ta'en or slain.

Brutus. Sit thee down, Clitus. Slaying is the word;
    It is a deed in fashion. Hark thee, Clitus.   5

                    [*Whispering.*]

Clitus. What, I, my lord? No, not for all the world.

Brutus. Peace, then, no words.

Clitus.   I'll rather kill myself.

Brutus. Hark thee, Dardanius!

Dardanius.   Shall I do such a deed?

Clitus. O Dardanius!

[77] *is chanc'd*: has unfolded.
[78] *poor remains*: bedraggled survivors.
[79] *Statilius show'd the torch-light . . . came not back*: According to Petrarch, Statilius volunteered for a reconnaissance mission and, arriving at Cassius' camp, signaled that all was well but then was captured.

Dardanius. O Clitus!   10

Clitus. What ill request did Brutus make to thee?

Dardanius. To kill him, Clitus. Look, he
     meditates.

Clitus. Now is that noble vessel[80] full of grief,
     That it runs over even at his eyes.

Brutus. Come hither, good Volumnius; list[81] a
     word.   15

Volumnius. What says my lord?

Brutus.   Why, this, Volumnius:
     The ghost of Caesar hath appear'd to me
     Two several[82] times by night—at Sardis once,
     And this last night here in Philippi fields.
     I know my hour is come.

Volumnius.   Not so, my lord.   20

Brutus. Nay, I am sure it is, Volumnius.
     Thou seest the world, Volumnius, how it goes:
     Our enemies have beat us to the pit;[83]

                              [*Low alarums.*]

     It is more worthy to leap in ourselves
     Than tarry till they push us. Good Volumnius,   25
     Thou know'st that we two went to school
          together;
     Even for that our love of old, I prithee,
     Hold thou my sword-hilts whilst I run on it.

[80] *vessel*: human being.
[81] *list*: hear.
[82] *several*: separate.
[83] *pit*: (1) pitfall, used to trap wild animals; (2) grave.

Volumnius. That's not an office for a friend, my
     lord.   [*Alarum still.*]

Clitus. Fly, fly, my lord; there is no tarrying
     here.   30

Brutus. Farewell to you; and you; and you,
     Volumnius.
   Strato, thou hast been all this while asleep;
   Farewell to thee too, Strato. Countrymen,
   My heart doth joy that yet in all my life
   I found no man but he was true to me.   35
   I shall have glory by this losing day,
   More than Octavius and Mark Antony
   By this vile conquest shall attain unto.
   So fare you well at once; for Brutus' tongue
   Hath almost ended his life's history.   40
   Night hangs upon mine eyes; my bones would
     rest,
   That have but labour'd to attain this hour.

               [*Alarum. Cry within, 'Fly, fly, fly!'*]

Clitus. Fly, my lord, fly.

Brutus.   Hence! I will follow.

        [*Exeunt Clitus, Dardanius, and Volumnius.*]

   I prithee, Strato, stay thou by thy lord;
   Thou art a fellow of a good respect;[84]   45
   Thy life hath had some smatch[85] of honour in it.
   Hold then my sword, and turn away thy face,
   While I do run upon it. Wilt thou, Strato?

Strato. Give me your hand first. Fare you well,
     my lord.

---

[84] *respect*: reputation.
[85] *smatch*: smack.

Brutus. Farewell, good Strato. Caesar, now be
     still.   50
    I kill'd not thee with half so good a will.

               [*He runs on his sword, and dies.*]

*Alarum. Retreat. Enter Octavius, Antony, Messala,
Lucilius, and the Army.*

Octavius. What man is that?

Messala. My master's man. Strato, where is thy
     master?

Strato. Free from the bondage you are in,
     Messala.
    The conquerors can but make a fire of him;   55
    For Brutus only overcame himself,
    And no man else hath honour by his death.

Lucilius. So Brutus should be found. I thank
     thee, Brutus,
    That thou hast prov'd Lucilius' saying true.[86]

Octavius. All that serv'd Brutus, I will entertain[87]
     them.   60
    Fellow, wilt thou bestow thy time with me?

Strato. Ay, if Messala will prefer[88] me to you.

Octavius. Do so, good Messala.

Messala. How died my master, Strato?

Strato. I held the sword, and he did run on it.   65

---

[86] *That thou . . . true*: refers to "He will be found like Brutus, like himself"
(5.4.25).
     [87] *entertain*: take into service.
     [88] *prefer*: recommend.

Messala. Octavius, then take him to follow thee,
   That did the latest[89] service to my master.

Antony. This was the noblest Roman of them all.
   All the conspirators save only he
   Did that they did in envy of great Caesar;   70
   He only in a general honest thought
   And common good to all made one of them.
   His life was gentle; and the elements
   So mix'd in him that Nature might stand up
   And say to all the world, 'This was a man!'   75

Octavius. According to his virtue let us use[90] him,
   With all respect and rites of burial.
   Within my tent his bones to-night shall lie,
   Most like a soldier, ordered honourably.
   So call the field to rest, and let's away   80
   To part[91] the glories of this happy day.   [*Exeunt.*]

[89] *latest*: final, last.
[90] *use*: treat.
[91] *part*: share, divide.

Contemporary Criticism

Julius Caesar on Film

James Bemis
California Political Review

To better understand Shakespeare's *Julius Caesar*, it is important to delve into the development and motivations of the play's main characters. This is an unusual drama for Shakespeare in a number of ways: there are no memorable females (unforgettable female characters are one of Shakespeare's specialties), there are no comic characters or interludes, and there is virtually no music (Brutus' attendant Lucius quickly falls asleep while singing). The play has a classical feel to it, akin to the bloody Roman dramas of Seneca, giving it grandeur but also a certain stiffness, due to its lack of romance and humor. *Julius Caesar*, then, is almost exclusively about the politics and ambitions of men in all their folly and shortsightedness.

The drama features four main characters: Julius Caesar, Brutus, Cassius, and Mark Antony. Let us examine the characteristics of each man.

Understanding the Main Characters

Julius Caesar

It is a mark of the exceptional skill and boldness of Shakespeare that he could create and dispose of the title character in a relatively few lines in the first half of a play. Julius Caesar appears in only three scenes (not counting his ghost near the end) and is killed in the beginning of the third act.

Caesar, of course, was one of the most important men who ever lived, greatly extending the reach of the Roman Empire, enriching the Roman citizenry by making some of them wealthy by ransoming captive people, defeating his great rival Pompey in battle, and writing two classic books that at one time every educated schoolboy had read. Yet Shakespeare makes this man, considered a near deity in Rome, human—very human, in fact.

To accomplish this, Shakespeare shows us both the public and the private sides of Caesar. Publicly, the man is vain, pompous, obnoxious, and self-important. He refers to himself in the third person ("Speak. Caesar is turn'd to hear" [1.2.17]),[1] brags about his courage and steadfastness ("... I am constant as the northern star, / Of whose true-fix'd and resting quality / There is no fellow in the firmament" [3.1.60]), and goes to the Senate on the fateful ides of March fully expecting to be crowned king.

On the other hand, the private Caesar is shown to be an astute judge of men, capable of developing a close friendship with the strong and loyal Antony and accurately sizing up Cassius. However, Caesar is also superstitious (he asks Antony to touch his wife Calphurnia during the Lupercal race to cure her of sterility, and he consults augurers to read animal entrails before going to the Senate), changes his mind twice about going to the Senate House, is deaf in one ear, cannot swim, and is subject to "the falling sickness" (1.2.253). Hardly a godlike figure.

Thus, the actor playing this role must combine the officiousness of the public Caesar with the vulnerability and insecurity of the private Caesar. Further, it is apparent that the tough-minded Antony truly loved his friend, meaning there was something lovable in the old emperor. All these aspects must be portrayed by the player in the title role—not an easy task.

Brutus

If there is a tragic hero in *Julius Caesar*, it is the noble but self-deluded Brutus. Brutus thinks of himself as honorable (a notion Antony utterly destroys in his funeral oration) when in reality he is stubborn and shortsighted, a poor judge of character, and a hopeless optimist. Interestingly, Shakespeare

[1] All quotations from *Julius Caesar* are from the edition published by Ignatius Press: *Julius Caesar*, ed. Joseph Pearce, Ignatius Critical Editions (San Francisco: Ignatius Press, 2012).

sanitizes the real Brutus. According to Plutarch, Shakespeare's source for the play, Brutus may have been Caesar's illegitimate son, which puts his role in Caesar's murder in a very different light. Additionally, Plutarch notes that Brutus' knife thrust was into Caesar's "privities", giving a whole new meaning to "the most unkindest cut of all" (3.2.183).

Brutus is one of Shakespeare's supremely conflicted characters, similar to Hamlet and to Macbeth before his fall. He envisions himself as honest and above the fray and likely would not have initiated the conspiracy had he not been "seduc'd" by Cassius to join (1.2.311). But once he commits to the scheme, he assumes a leadership role—even a dominating one—and rationalizes the assassination until the very end.

Commentators disagree whether Brutus is a noble victim of circumstance or a delusional fool who, because of his shortsightedness, inadvertently brings disaster upon his nation and countrymen. These views are colored in part by whether the author sees the Roman conspiracy as an attempt to prevent tyranny or as an assassination by violent revolutionaries attempting to usurp rightful authority.

Cassius

In a lesser playwright's hands, Cassius would be the simple villain of the drama, the seducer of Brutus who leads the protagonist to his downfall, and the agent of the tragedy that befalls all Romans. But Shakespeare is a master of character and is not content with creating stock players. He gives Cassius a number of virtues and even some endearing physical flaws (such as nearsightedness), and both his virtues and his flaws help expedite his tragic end. He is a master manipulator and a fomenter of rebellion, an excellent judge of men who seems to know exactly what strategy to use to lure others into the conspiracy, appealing to Brutus' enlarged sense of honor and Casca's inferiority complex, for example.

Cassius seems to know instinctively that Brutus cannot be argued into joining the conspiracy but must convince him to go along by "indirection" (cf. 4.3.75). In Act 1, scene 2, Cassius first reminds Brutus that Caesar is just a man like the two of them—he is a poor swimmer and cries like a girl when he is sick (1.2.97–131). Then, in a masterstroke, he appeals to Brutus' sense of honor by reminding him of his illustrious ancestor who drove the Tarquin king out of Rome. From that moment on, Brutus is hooked.

Yet, despite manipulating others to achieve his own ends, Cassius proves a steadfast, loyal friend to Brutus, although his acquiescence in Brutus' idealism proves disastrous. Thus, the actor playing Cassius must be credible as a cynical manipulator but also softhearted enough to be the accommodating and sympathetic friend of Brutus. Part villain, part codependent enabler, the role of Cassius is subtle and nuanced, and so must be the dramatic performance.

Mark Antony

Mark Antony is the drama's strongest force and is given some of the play's most memorable lines. He is the primal power who will foil the conspirators' best laid plans. Like all the play's main characters, he has two distinct sides to his personality: he is a warmhearted and friendly man, yet also a cold-blooded killer; a fun-loving partier, yet a tough-minded soldier; a self-described "plain blunt man" (3.2.218), yet a brilliant orator.

The actor playing Mark Antony carries a heavy burden: his performance can make or break a production. He is a very strong character who dominates the play from the third act on. Yet there are touches of grace and humility in him that require great nuance. It is a difficult role, and not many pull it off successfully.

Julius Caesar on Film: Three Performances

A few performances of *Julius Caesar* are available on film. Let us look at how the characters are developed in three productions. The results are summarized in table 1.

1: Summary of Three Film Productions of *Julius Caesar*

Year Produced	1953	1970	1979
Director	Joseph Mankiewicz	Stuart Burge	Herbert Wise
Casting:			
Caesar	Louis Calhern	John Gielgud	Charles Gray
Brutus	James Mason	Jason Robards	Richard Pasco
Cassius	John Gielgud	Richard Johnson	David Collings
Mark Antony	Marlon Brando	Charlton Heston	Keith Michell
Act 1, Scene 2: Caesar's Entrance; Cassius' "Seduction" of Brutus	Haughty Caesar well played; Gielgud particularly effective as Cassius	Gielgud masterful; Robards disastrous as Brutus	Gray's Caesar appropriately self-important and condescending
Act 2, Scene 1: Brutus Joins the Conspiracy	Mason's methodical style serves the role of Brutus well	Robards has all the expression of a corpse; Johnson's energetic, angry Cassius works well	Pasco's Brutus is too aloof and unsympathetic
Act 2, Scene 2: Caesar Decides to Go to the Senate	Calphurnia's role overacted, but innocent Caesar heightens suspense	Caesar's vulnerability portrayed effectively	Caesar's doubts underplayed; necessary vulnerability lacking
Act 3, Scene 1: Caesar's Assassination and the Aftermath	Most moving scene in the film; Brutus' indecisive character highlighted	Brutus is lethargic, seems to lack energy enough to deliver "most unkindest cut"	Carried off well, if stagey
Act 3, Scene 2: Funeral Orations	Mason's Brutus flat and unemotional, but Brando as Antony a revelation with perfect delivery	Robards utterly forgettable; Heston marginally better	Disastrous scene: Brutus lifeless, Antony a lightweight
Act 4, Scene 1: Rome's New Order	Brando chilling	Loses meaning due to director's choice to have scene in a spa	Michell's Antony lacks menacing quality
Act 4, Scene 3: Quarrel in the Tent	Both old pros good, but Gielgud acquires audience's sympathy	Only scene where Robards performs well, as does Johnson	Well done, with Collings particularly good
Act 5, Scene 5: Brutus' Eulogy	Homage to Brutus desultory	Antony's speech flat and unmoving	Eulogy flat, more mean than magnanimous
Overall Grade	B	C+	D+

Metro-Goldwyn-Mayer (MGM) (1953)

The granddaddy of all the film versions of Julius Caesar is MGM's 1953 production, directed by Joseph L. Mankiewicz, winner of best director Oscars for *All About Eve* and *A Letter to Three Wives*. The movie was nominated for five Academy Awards (best picture, best actor, best cinematography, best music, and best art direction), winning for best art direction. The film, a staple of high school English classes, stars Louis Calhern as Caesar, James Mason as Brutus, John Gielgud as Cassius, and Marlon Brando as Antony.

Overall, this version is solid, with strong production values and a renowned cast. As cinema, though, it is somewhat stiff and lifeless. Some reviewers believe that Brando was woefully miscast as Antony, but I disagree. The young Brando possessed a latent animal strength and magnetism, exactly what this production otherwise lacks. One senses these same qualities in the character Shakespeare drew, making Brando a fine casting fit.

In Act 1, scene 2, we get our first glimpse of the imperious and haughty Caesar, well played by Louis Calhern. Two old pros, Gielgud and Mason, acquit themselves admirably as Cassius and Brutus, respectively. Gielgud is particularly effective in this early scene as he skulks furtively around, clearly envious of the great Caesar. When Caesar notes to Antony, "Yond Cassius has a lean and hungry look" (1.2.194), the camera pans up to Cassius on the balustrade above, and Gielgud's look is not only lean and hungry but furtive as a rat too, adding to the richness of the scene.

James Mason's methodical, thoughtful acting style benefits the role of Brutus. In Act 2, scene 1, the naïve high-mindedness of Brutus is evident in Mason's bland visage as the conspirators lay out their plans. Gielgud's Cassius is particularly good in this scene: he is crafty enough to organize the conspiracy and accurately size up Antony but shows his fatal weakness by deferring to his friend Brutus.

Act 2, scene 2, concentrates on Caesar and his wife Calphurnia, played by Greer Garson, who horribly overacts.

Caesar's wavering over whether to go to the Senate House is made believable by Calhern, and his innocent and naïve welcoming of the conspirators heightens the film's suspense.

The play's first half climaxes with Caesar's murder in Act 3, scene 1. An interesting insight into Brutus' indecisive character is added by director Mankiewicz: on several occasions (with Cassius, with Portia, with the blind Soothsayer, and with the wounded Caesar), Brutus backs up and then turns away when confronted by others. Calhern's acting when he realizes his friend has also betrayed him ("Et tu, Brute?" [3.1.77]) is the most moving moment in the film, and the audience cannot help but turn against the conspirators from that moment on.

Act 3, scene 2, is highlighted, of course, by the funeral orations of Brutus and Cassius. Mason's speech is flat, rational, and unemotionally delivered, as befits the man. Brando's delivery of Antony's speech, however, is a revelation: he starts slowly, but as the rage within him builds, he speaks louder and with more emphasis. With each repetition of the word "honorable" applied to the conspirators, his face becomes more sneering and sarcastic. When he utters his last words and the crowd descends into chaos and destruction, we see by his sardonic smile that he is well satisfied with the mayhem he has created.

In Act 4, scene 1, we see that Antony has become the cold, ruthless dictator the conspirators feared Caesar would be. Brando is excellent here, and the effect of him seating himself in Caesar's throne is chilling.

In Act 4, scene 3, Brutus and Cassius verbally battle it out in a tent. True to form, Mason is coolly rational, refusing to lose his temper, even when insulted. Gielgud, conversely, perfectly captures Cassius' rage and then quickly cools down when he learns of his friend's loss of his wife. By the scene's end, he is both forgiving and forgiven. These human qualities are expertly drawn out by Gielgud, and we feel more sympathy for Cassius than Brutus as a result.

Antony's desultory homage to Brutus in Act 5, scene 5, ends the production. Overall, the MGM film is adequate, even exceptional at times, due to Brando's inspired performance, if a bit yawn inspiring and lackluster in parts.

Commonwealth United Entertainment
and Republic Pictures (1970)

In 1970 Commonwealth United Entertainment, in conjunction with Republic Pictures, released a production of *Julius Caesar*. The film, directed by Stuart Burge, starred John Gielgud as Caesar, Jason Robards as Brutus, Richard Johnson as Cassius, and Charlton Heston as Mark Antony.

Gielgud, of course, is one of the great Shakespearean actors of our time, and his Caesar here is done effectively. Supremely confident yet displaying a hint of vulnerability, Gielgud is masterful in the opening scene. The veteran Robards, on the other hand, is an unmitigated disaster. His Brutus moves through scenes with all the expression of a corpse, and not even the beautiful Diana Rigg as Portia, wonderful in her big scene in Act 2, scene 1, can bring the comatose actor to life. One wonders where Robards finds the energy to deliver "the most unkindest cut of all" when slaying Caesar in Act 3, scene 1.

Richard Johnson's Cassius, on the other hand, is very effective—full of energy and anger. The envious, spiteful side of Cassius is played up, and his utter disdain for Caesar in Act 1, scene 2, comes through loud and clear. No ambiguous motives here—this Cassius hates Caesar's guts!

Moving on to the big funeral orations in Act 3, scene 2, Robards' speech is utterly forgettable, done in a low-key professional manner, in keeping with the rest of his undistinguished performance. Heston's speech as Antony is marginally better, for although Heston lacks superior acting ability, he is animated and sincere in his performance, which is more than you can say for Robards.

For some reason, director Burge has Act 4, scene 1, where the new triumvirate is deciding the lives and deaths of Rome's citizens, take place in a spa, where Octavius and Antony are getting massages. This off-putting scene rubs viewers the wrong way and robs the action of much of its unnerving nature. Antony comes off not so much as a merciless tyrant as a football coach picking his starting lineup.

The "quarrel in the tent" scene (Act 4, scene 3) is the only one in which Robards performs at the level at which he is capable. He is fine here, as is Johnson's Cassius, and the scene is moving and edifying in revealing much about the men's characters. The battle scenes attempt to be epic but are neither choreographed well enough to be interesting nor bloody enough to be realistic. Antony's final speech in Act 5, scene 5, is flat and unmoving, but whether this is because of Heston's shallowness or our lack of empathy for Robard's Brutus is difficult to tell.

British Broadcasting Corporation (BBC) (1979)

As part of its Complete Dramatic Works of William Shakespeare series, the BBC produced a film version of *Julius Caesar* in 1979, directed by television veteran Herbert Wise. The cast included Charles Gray as Caesar, Richard Pasco as Brutus, David Collings as Cassius, and Keith Michell as Mark Antony.

In Act 1, scene 2, we meet the main cast and quickly sense that something is amiss, as several of the major players are miscast, unusual for this usually top-notch BBC series. Keith Michell is a weak, rather effete Antony, and it is difficult to see him posing a threat to anyone. Richard Pasco plays Brutus in a rather monochromatic fashion, seemingly without any inner doubts about what he is doing. The focal point of this scene, though, is Charles Gray's Caesar, who is supremely self-important and condescending. David Collings makes a fine Cassius, shrewd yet vulnerable.

In Act 2, scene 1, we get deep into Brutus' character. Here one of this production's shortcomings becomes evident: Pasco is too aloof and unsympathetic to gain our empathy. When Brutus meets with the conspirators, it does not seem credible that such a lethargic character could take charge of the group. His important scene with Portia is played superficially and without emotion despite its being one of the few scenes where Shakespeare allows Brutus to let his hair down.

Caesar's doubts about going to the Senate House are underplayed in Act 2, scene 2. Gray's Caesar is long on pomposity but short on vulnerability, something Shakespeare added to show a more human side of Caesar. Despite the cheap production budget, Caesar's murder in Act 3, scene 1, is carried off well, if it is a bit stagey.

This production's problems come to the forefront in the great funeral orations in Act 3, scene 2. Brutus' mechanical, methodical speech seems to be given by rote, as Pasco takes Brutus' Stoicism to be lifelessness, which is not the same thing as Stoicism at all. Michell is even worse: his Antony is a lightweight, missing the ferocity crucial to the role. Antony's funeral oration lacks resonance and gravity, and portions of it border on camp. It is hard to imagine anyone taking to the streets after listening to such a flaccid performance.

Likewise, in Act 4, scene 1, this Antony is without the menace proper to the scene as Michell, the older man, is overshadowed by Octavius, the younger one. The quarrel in the tent in Act 4, scene 3, is well done, with Collings particularly good as the mercurial Cassius, ready to kill, to be killed, and then to comfort his friend in rapid succession. Such a change of moods is difficult to pull off well, and Collings does a fine job of it.

Casting a cipher like Michell undermines the final scene of Antony's eulogy of Brutus. What should have been magnanimity comes across as meanness, and the entire production ends on a flat note. All in all, this film is a less-than-inspired performance by the usually reliable BBC.

Conclusion

Few would consider *Julius Caesar* to be one of Shakespeare's greatest tragedies, compared to *Hamlet*, *Othello*, *King Lear*, *Macbeth*, or *Romeo and Juliet*. Nevertheless, it is a play with many great moments, memorable lines, and lessons that stretch over the sands of time.

Caesar's assassination was one of the most famous events in history. Shakespeare's dramatization of it provokes two important questions: Was Caesar's assassination morally justified? Was it politically justified?

Shakespeare never directly answers these questions, but one gets a sense of the playwright's perspective by how the drama unfolds after Caesar's murder: Rome succumbs to a brutal civil war, the conspirators' side ends in death and defeat, both Brutus and Cassius commit suicide, and the Romans fall under a tyranny far worse than Caesar's. In short, Brutus' hopeless idealism led to disaster at every turn, and his rival Mark Antony emerged ultimately triumphant.

As a lesson in the unintended consequences of idealism in politics and the narrow limitations of man's rational capacity, art has few parallels to *Julius Caesar*. Yet a great film version of the play has yet to be made. Compared to the others, however, the 1953 Joseph Mankiewicz version, with an electric performance by Marlon Brando as Mark Antony and a solid performance by James Mason as the brooding Brutus, at least provides a good sense of Shakespeare's overarching theme of the unpredictability of the outcomes of war and revolution. If only modern leaders were grounded in this insightful drama, much of the world's mischief could be avoided.

Brutus and the Art of Misconstruction

Michael Hanke

Julius Caesar has been termed a problem play encompassing
"the psychological problem of the nature of the 'real' Caesar",
"the moral problem of the justification of the murder", and
the authorial problem "that Shakespeare deliberately avoided
giving a plain and clear-cut answer to either of these problems".[1] Regarding the last of these quotations, it has to be
pointed out that nowhere in his mature plays does Shakespeare tend to state his personal opinions, much less preach.
He presents us with a problem and leaves it at that. However
much scholars have striven to offer a conspectus of his con-
victions, we are left with no more than "a commonplace of
Shakespeare criticism: that his beliefs cannot be ascertained,
that he has no 'message' or doctrine, but makes us face the
same problems which we have to deal with when contemplating history or mankind in general".[2] *Julius Caesar*, with its companion pieces *Antony and Cleopatra* and *Coriolanus*, is based
on Sir Thomas North's translation of Bishop Jacques Amyot's
French version of Plutarch's *Lives of the Noble Grecians and
Romans*. Plot and character in these plays clearly indicate that
Shakespeare found himself in perfect agreement with Plutarch in "envisioning human beings as fluctuating crowds on
a fairground".[3] This precludes any kind of simple message
hunting.

---

[1] Ernest Schanzer, *The Problem Plays of Shakespeare* (London: Routledge and
Kegan Paul, 1963), p. 70.

[2] Johannes Kleinstück, "The Problem of Order in Shakespeare's Histories",
Neophilologus 38 (1954): 268. See the same critic's "Ulysses' Speech on Degree
as Related to the Play of *Troilus and Cressida*", *Neophilologus* 43 (1959): 111–18.

[3] See Rudolf Sühnel's "Plutarch, Klassiker der Biographie, und seine Über-
setzer Jacques Amyot (1559) und Sir Thomas North (1579)", in *Biographie zwis-
chen Renaissance und Barock: Zwölf Studien*, ed. Walter Berschin (Heidelberg:
Mattes, 1993), pp. 129–56.

Quite apart from the difficulties of character assessment, the play reflects for modern audiences the controversial appraisal of the historical personalities of Brutus and Caesar. Dante condemned Brutus (with Judas) to eternal perdition, while on the other hand, he was stylized a hero of freedom by Enlightenment rationalists struggling against eighteenth-century absolutism. Caesar, like Napoleon, has been seen as either despot or "history on horseback".[4] More than scrupulous character analysis on moral grounds, this constantly shifting ideological background has led critics to come down resolutely on the side of either Brutus or Caesar.

The play's opening scene delineates the difficulties of forming a definite impression of the title hero. At first the streets are abuzz with cheerful plebeians; toward the end of the scene, the crowd is almost dispersed. Gaiety is succeeded by consternation. Expecting Caesar's return and celebration of his defeat of Pompey, which has ended a threat to political stability, the common people have gotten a day off and throng the stage. They are, however, sternly berated by the tribunes Flavius and Marullus for supporting a tyrant after having cheered Pompey for better reasons. Flavius' impression that the crowd slinks away deeply moved is, however, no more than wishful thinking. In fact, it seems that the common people do not share the tribunes' belief that Caesar is a tyrant:

> Unlike the Plebeian in *Coriolanus*, they have no grievance. They seem to be quite happy, and fairly prosperous; only eager, like the good fellows they are, "to get themselves into more work". There is no sign that they feel themselves to be victims of any sort of oppression, and evidently the notion that there is anything unworthy in acquiescence in a rule that is merely righteous (we have Brutus' testimony that it is righteous) is a political conception far beyond them.... They are not

[4] See Friedrich Gundolf's *Caesar: Geschichte seines Ruhms* (Berlin: Bondi, 1924) and his discussion of *Julius Caesar* in *Shakespeare: Sein Wesen und Werk*, vol. 1 (Berlin: Bondi, 1928), pp. 5–46.

"politically minded", but they genuinely admire their country's
great one, and are hero-worshippers to a man.[5]

The tribunes' scorn suggests that it is not Caesar but his accus-
ers, driven by envy, who obstruct natural order, foreshadowing
the nasty turn the story will take when Brutus concludes that
his friend is "a serpent's egg" (2.1.32).[6] The introductory
scene offers the first of a series of portraits, none of which gives
a clear picture of Caesar as a public and a private man. Plutarch, on the other hand, loses no time in turning against Caesar.
Shakespeare's shift away from a simple black-and-white portrait lends verisimilitude to Caesar and, later on, to Brutus.

Nor does Caesar appear as a murderous tyrant in the long
second scene when, to the sound of drums and trumpets, he
passes by in procession. Certain humanizing factors have been
ignored by critics bent on elevating the moral status of his
murderer:

> His personal presence seems comparatively undramatic.... At
> any rate, he hardly strikes us as a dangerous tyrant or a villain
> consumed by ambition.... The fact that he is deaf in one ear—a
> handicap added by Shakespeare—and troubled with the "fall-
> ing sickness" does not mean that the dramatist deliberately
> reduced his heroic stature, but rather underlines the extraor-
> dinary force of his presence which is not even impaired by these
> physical defects. Nor will Cassius' tales about Caesar's weak-
> ness convince us that his authority is mere sham because they
> are so obviously dictated by hatred and envy and say more about
> the speaker himself than about the man he wants to belittle.[7]

There is little more to be said about Caesar's character. The
most convincing, and convenient, way of defending Caesar

[5] Sir Mark Hunter, "Brutus and the Political Context" (1931), in *Shakespeare:
"Julius Caesar"—A Casebook*, ed. Peter Ure (London: Macmillan, 1969), p. 199.
This has been called "surely one of the best essays on the play" (J. I. M. Stewart).

[6] All quotations from *Julius Caesar* are from the edition published by Ignatius
Press: *Julius Caesar*, ed. Joseph Pearce, Ignatius Critical Editions (San Francisco:
Ignatius Press, 2012).

[7] Dieter Mehl, *Shakespeare's Tragedies: An Introduction* (Cambridge: Cambridge University Press, 1986), pp. 135–36.

may be found in Cassius' monologue, where he passes judgment on Brutus, and in Brutus' own monologue, where he pains-
takingly pieces together arguments in favor of what he has
already decided to classify not as murder but as tyrannicide.

Cassius, after tempting Brutus to consider a number of
absurdly contrived reasons for getting rid of Caesar, knowing
only too well that they are all motivated by envy and hatred,
has this to say of his future fellow combatant:

> Well, Brutus, thou art noble; yet, I see,
> Thy honourable mettle may be wrought
> From that it is dispos'd. Therefore it is meet
> That noble minds keep ever with their likes;
> For who so firm that cannot be seduc'd?
> Caesar doth bear me hard; but he loves Brutus.
> If I were Brutus now and he were Cassius,
> He should not humour me.
>
>   (1.2.307–14)

If we take into account that Brutus will later fly into a fury
over Cassius' crime of extortion, Cassius here utters a far more
damning pronouncement. Brutus seriously considers, and later
carries out, the betrayal of a friend, which causes Cassius to
despise him and Dante to consign him to Hell.

Cassius' short monologue foreshadows what is to come. There
is no excuse for Brutus' course of action, and it is this fatal
lack of mental stability that so signally sets him off from Caesar,
whose slightly pompous but accurate self-assessment shows that
he, not Brutus, is the true representative of *constantia*: "I could
be well mov'd, if I were as you . . . /But I am constant as the
northern star" (3.1.58–60). And these words are spoken in a
context indicating that Caesar senses the same instability in
Brutus that he had reason to observe in Cassius (cf. 1.2.192ff.).
That Brutus' mettle has already been wrought from "that it is
dispos'd" is brought home to us in what must be one of the
most brilliantly worded self-deceptions in drama, a Shakespearean masterpiece of psychological realism:

It must be by his death; and for my part,
I know no personal cause to spurn at him,
But for the general: he would be crown'd.
How that might change his nature, there's the question.
It is the bright day that brings forth the adder,
And that craves wary walking. Crown him—that!
And then, I grant, we put a sting in him
That at his will he may do danger with.
Th' abuse of greatness is, when it disjoins
Remorse from power; and to speak truth of Caesar,
I have not known when his affections sway'd
More than his reason. But 'tis a common proof
That lowliness is young ambition's ladder,
Whereto the climber-upward turns his face;
But when he once attains the upmost round,
He then unto the ladder turns his back,
Looks in the clouds, scorning the base degrees
By which he did ascend. So Caesar may.
Then, lest he may, prevent. And since the quarrel
Will bear no colour for the thing he is,
Fashion it thus—that what he is, augmented,
Would run to these and these extremities;
And therefore think him as a serpent's egg,
Which, hatch'd, would as his kind grow mischievous,
And kill him in the shell.

(2.1.10–34)

We find Brutus too busy piling hypothesis upon hypothesis
to analyze the line of reasoning that he takes as a bedrock
foundation for his *idée fixe* (Cassius-born) that Caesar has to
be killed. Let us have a look at just a few of his statements.
"[H]e would be crown'd": This can hardly be said to be a fact.
What we have to go on is nothing but Casca's words, who
according to Brutus himself is a "blunt fellow" (1.2.294). The
hypothesis needs to be added to, and Brutus does not hesi-
tate to do so by assuming that, if Caesar were to become king,
his character would change. Brutus is only fleetingly aware

that he does not and cannot know what the results of that change, should it occur at all, might be. Nevertheless, it seems safest to him to assume the worst, and with breathtaking non-chalance Brutus dehumanizes his friend by imagining him as a snake. Lost in his fantasy, Brutus is unable to see that it was Cassius who put a sting into him that indeed will "do danger" not only to Caesar but to the commonwealth. The ladder image is suggestive less of Caesar's political plans than those of Brutus.

Brutus' *conclusio* ("It must be by his death") is tellingly placed at the beginning, not the end, of his *argumentatio*. He is as confident of his course of action as he is uncertain of its jus-tification. His imagination surrogates moral reasoning. It is no wonder that, unassailed by doubt and unafraid of being con-tradicted by Cassius, Brutus later justifies the assassination by accusing his victim of having supported "robbers" (4.3.23). That is Brutus all over, his powers of repression permitting him to remain blissfully unaware of having formerly admitted that he had not known that Caesar's "affections sway'd / More than his reason" (2.1.20–21). With such textual evidence, it is hard not to believe that Brutus' honesty, on which his reputation of nobility so largely rests, is the result of his complete mis-construction of self. Of all Shakespearean characters, he is the most expert at nipping in the bud the slightest stirring of self-doubt.

Caesar's claims to being a tragic figure are fairly slight:

> The life of Caesar did not afford the stuff out of which an effective play can be constructed. Hence it is not the life, but the death of Julius, which is the central and all-controlling theme of the tragedy; the death of Caesar, the circumstances leading to, attending and resulting from it; how also several persons, greatly endowed, but not quite rising to fully tragic dimensions, were affected by it. There is truth, therefore, in the old gibe that in the play of *Julius Caesar* the eponymous hero is brought upon the stage merely to be killed.[8]

[8] Hunter, "Brutus and the Political Context", pp. 196–97.

But neither are the other characters, including Brutus, of truly tragic dimension. Let us apply Aristotelian terminology to trace more clearly the tragic substance of Shakespeare's hero.[9] In Brutus' case there is no *catharsis* or purification, nor can there be, for the simple reason that he does not, in the end, achieve *anagnorisis* in the sense of self-knowledge. The errors and crimes he has committed (*hamartia*) are not, for him, brought into focus. This explains why he never abandons his air of stultifying innocence: ". . . I am arm'd so strong in honesty" (4.3.67). Had we not witnessed the murderous activities that led Rome to a brutal civil war, we might almost believe him, but when he lords his supposedly superior morals over Cassius without realizing that he himself had longed to profit from the crimes he now so self-righteously castigates, we are less inclined to do so.

It is Brutus' almost total inability to drag himself by will-power to even a modicum of self-knowledge that sets him so far apart from the self-searching heroes of Shakespeare's mature tragedies. Whereas the lives of the latter at some predestined point in the play explode into meaning, or absurdity (as with Macbeth), Brutus manages to muddle through by keeping a stiff upper lip and on the strength of his Stoicism, as evidenced in his manly reaction to Portia's suicide (in Act 4, scene 3). His subconscious sense of guilt, almost tangible in the revelatory flash of Caesar's appearance before the battle of Philippi ("Thy evil spirit" [4.3.279]), leaves him only momentarily dazed rather than permanently enlightened.

In *Julius Caesar* Shakespeare, whatever else he may be up to, certainly does not preach the Tudor doctrine of order, though the need for constitutional and moral stability are strongly implied by the motifs of insubordination, dishonesty, and self-deception and by the use of the storm as a suggestive prelude to Caesar's assassination. And yet readers and viewers may inadvertently slip into the position of shortsighted Cassius, who,

[9] For definitions of the following literary terms, see M. H. Abrams, *A Glossary of Literary Terms*, 3rd ed. (New York: Holt, Rinehart and Winston, 1971).

scorning Caesar's all-too-human deficiencies, sends his friend Titinius to find out if some troops seen in the distance are friends or foes, and orders Pindarus to watch him from a hill to report on his progress. When Pindarus sees Titinius suddenly surrounded by a group of wild horsemen, he assumes them to be enemies. On hearing this, Cassius is deeply shaken and commands Pindarus to help him commit suicide. His death, in a way, is the result of getting it all wrong by not being able to use his own eyes and brains. Titinius, however, gets it right when contemplating his friend's death: "Alas, thou hast misconstrued every thing!" (5.3.84). His words not only contain an element of poetic justice but also point to the danger of misconstruing oneself and the world, a danger to which all the major characters are prone: "Indeed, it is a strange-disposed time;/But men may construe things after their fashion,/Clean from the purpose of the things themselves" (1.3.33–35).

These words are Cicero's response to Casca's hysterical account of the thunderstorm sweeping the capital. Above self-deception, Cicero knows that signs may be read in very different ways, each interpretation depending on subconscious desires and needs:

> Cicero—the historical Cicero—was an exponent of academic and philosophical scepticism. Shakespeare seems to have known this, for he has him answer as a sceptic—and react so as well, for Cicero, after his fashion, dispenses with all interpretation of the event and goes home.... In this scene we find three distinct interpretations of the storm and its omens, each corresponding to a different fashion and thus exposing the speaker's character.[10]

All the major characters mistake wishful thinking for fact: Brutus is so convinced of Antony's harmlessness that he waves aside Cassius' well-founded warnings; Caesar disregards various

[10] Johannes Kleinstück, *Mythos und Symbol in englischer Dichtung* (Stuttgart: Kohlhammer, 1964), p. 111.

warnings that his life is in danger; and Antony even assures
Caesar that Cassius is not dangerous.

This habit of misconstruction is less important to the con-
ception of Caesar and Antony because—up to Caesar's fall—
they lack tragic stature. Though Brutus is the character that
comes closest to a tragic hero, it is not he who makes the play
so fascinating. It is Shakespeare, who on reading Plutarch rel-
ished the prospect of recreating the vanguard of Roman republicanism as an addled old Stoic. Shakespeare questions Plutarch's
sober defense of a man who, on closer inspection, simply will
not do as a model of the Roman virtues of *virtus, constantia,
fides,* and *sapientia.* Shakespeare again transcends the mental
powers of his dramatic characters. If Brutus is unwilling to
appreciate the horrors resulting from his *hamartia,* Shakespeare was all the more aware of them. Regan's impertinent
characterization of her father in *King Lear* fits Brutus to a T:
"[Y]et he hath ever but slenderly known himself." [11] The only
insight Shakespeare grants Brutus is the vague idea, pervading
the final act, that *after* (certainly not before) the assassination
of Caesar, something must have gone terribly wrong in Rome.
He comes to the resigned realization that Caesar is "mighty
yet" (5.3.94) and that his own "hour is come" (5.5.20).

To dwell on the negative traits in Brutus is not to deny him
the measure of humanity so apparent in his talk with Portia
and in the way he deals with young Lucius. However, Brutus'
long garden soliloquy and, even before that, Cassius' cutting
remark on Brutus' gullibility show, once for all, that under analysis the moral problem of the justification of murder vanishes
into thin air. Shakespeare, as *anima naturaliter dramatica,* does
not pontificate on the matter and permits us to draw our own
conclusions. The fairest characterization of Brutus may be that

> while he is himself inconsistent, even so does he suffer his asso-
> ciates, unreproved, to speak and act in glaring contradiction
> of the pure and lofty protestations with which he is always

[11] William Shakespeare, *King Lear,* ed. Joseph Pearce, Ignatius Critical Editions (San Francisco: Ignatius Press, 2008), 1.1.295.

ready. Cassius can pour into his ear, unchecked, dispraise of Caesar, inspired plainly by mere envy and spite. Caius Ligarius is welcomed as a confederate in an enterprise, pronounced to be free from all taint of personal malice, on the ground that he bears Caesar a grudge. One need not recall the treachery of Decius and Trebonius, evil means to an evil end, but approved by Brutus. His own conduct, apart from the capital crime, is sometimes at strange variance with principles simultaneously professed.[12]

Though Brutus is a tragic figure because of his *hamartia* and his violent death in the final act, the central tragedy of the play itself (it is, after all, a political play) is not to be found in Brutus' character but in the paradox that his unique art of misconstruction in the end brings about what he so fervently wants to forestall—civil war, the death of those dearest to him, and as shown by the facts of Roman history, political tyranny. He might almost be regarded as a test case for moral rectitude.

[12] Hunter, "Brutus and the Political Context", p. 204.

Supporting Robbers:
The Economic Conflict in *Julius Caesar*

James E. Hartley
Mount Holyoke College

The modern reader often has a difficult time separating prior beliefs about the assassination of Julius Caesar from the moral tale being told by Shakespeare. In fact, it is not entirely obvious what we think about the historical assassination. On one side, we have Dante, who places Brutus and Cassius in the lowest circle of Hell, eternally being chewed by Satan. Their company in this torment is none other than Judas Iscariot.[1] On the other side, we have Joseph Addison's *Cato*, a play beloved by the American Founding Fathers for its unstinting portrayal of Caesar as a tyrant, being opposed by heroic Romans proclaiming, "It is not a time to talk of aught / But chains or conquest, liberty or death."[2] Thoughts on Caesar have divided in this manner since the time of his assassination. Was he a tyrant, deserving of death? Or was he a good ruler, slain by vain, ambitious, envious men? Our view of Caesar is confused.

But what of Shakespeare's play? Is it in the tradition of Dante in condemning the conspirators? Or is it the model from which Addison and others like him draw their moral? Who is the hero of this play? Is it Caesar, for whom the play is named but who dies at the halfway mark? Is it Antony, the defender of Caesar and ultimate victor? Or is it Cassius and Brutus, who slay Caesar but are undone at the end? If this is a tragedy, who is the tragic figure?

Before looking at Shakespeare's play, it is useful to consider what motivated the historical conspirators. Although

---

[1] Dante, *Inferno* 34.27–69.

[2] Joseph Addison, *Cato: A Tragedy and Selected Essays*, ed. Christine Dunn Henderson and Mark E. Yellin (Indianapolis: Liberty Fund, 2004), 2.4.79–80.

Shakespeare's Antony hints that they were simply envious of Caesar, they did have a more tangible incentive. Caesar, since his first entry into politics, had joined in the latest round of a long-running conflict in Rome. In the centuries leading up to Caesar's reign, the Roman aristocracy had fought repeated battles over the distribution of wealth in the Roman Republic.[3] Previous leaders of the republic had split, sometimes violently, over this question. On the one side, there was always a large segment of the aristocracy who disliked the commoners. The sentiments of these aristocrats are perhaps best expressed by Shakespeare himself, when he has Coriolanus, who epitomized this view, say:

For the mutable, rank-scented many, let them
Regard me as I do not flatter, and
Therein behold themselves: I say again,
In soothing them, we nourish 'gainst our senate
The cockle of rebellion, insolence, sedition,
Which we ourselves have plough'd for, sow'd, and scatter'd,
By mingling them with us, the honour'd number;
Who lack not virtue, no, nor power, but that
Which they have given to beggars.[4]

The other side was epitomized by Tiberius and Gaius Gracchus, populists who pushed through a wide array of measures to redistribute wealth toward the poor. The policies advocated by the Gracchi caused a permanent split in Roman politics between the *populares*, who wanted to curry favor with the plebeians, and the *optimates*, who supported the traditional role of the aristocracy. This battle over economic policy was part and parcel of the political intrigue of the Roman Republic. On the one hand, currying favor with the masses by populist measures was a sure way to look strong, but on the

---

[3] For a useful summary of the structure of the economy in Rome, see Peter Temin, "The Economy of the Early Roman Empire", *Journal of Economic Perspectives* 21 (2006): 133–51.

[4] William Shakespeare, *Coriolanus*, ed. Tom Crawford (Mineola, New York: Dover, 2003), 3.1.84–92.

other hand, the masses were undoubtedly fickle. Shakespeare beautifully captures the fickleness of the crowd at Caesar's funeral. After Brutus' oration we find the plebeians yelling that Brutus deserves great honors, but within sixty lines the crowd has turned against him. (The crowd in *Coriolanus* acts in the same manner.)

Throughout his political career, Caesar had a strategy that was in alignment with the *populares*. Caesar was first elected as consul in 59 B.C. but was in Rome for only a brief time before leaving to conquer Gaul. In the next fifteen years, he was rarely in the capital itself, spending much of that time in Gaul, fighting Pompey in the civil war, and then involved in Egyptian politics with Cleopatra. He finally returned to Rome in triumph in 45 B.C., only to be assassinated in 44 B.C.

Despite spending so little time off the battlefield, Caesar was remarkably active in trying to shape the Roman economy to his liking. Immediately after first becoming consul, Caesar pushed through a land reform bill, giving land not only to ex-soldiers but also to the landless poor citizens of Rome. Caesar kept extending the scope of this reform throughout his career. His purpose is nicely illustrated in the case of the region of Buthrotum:

> But Cicero's friend Atticus, who was patron of that region, complained to Caesar about the confiscations which the scheme would necessitate. On the characteristic condition that he should receive compensation in cash from the wealthy Atticus, Caesar agreed to waive the plan. But then Cicero was much surprised to learn that the prospective settlers, starting out for their new homes, had not been told that these had vanished into thin air. Caesar, taxed with this failure to inform them, was reported to have explained "that he did not want to upset the people, while they were still in Rome—for, as you know, he aims at popularity—but when they were across the Adriatic he would see to it that they were transferred to some other territory." [5]

[5] Michael Grant, *Julius Caesar* (New York: McGraw Hill, 1969), p. 236.

Caesar's populist reforms were not limited to giving land to the poor, however. He also waded into the mire of financial reform. This was not a task for a timid reformer because "the financial intrigues of the declining Republic were complex, and often unsavory."[6] To alter this situation, Caesar canceled all interest payments due since the beginning of the civil war, causing creditors to lose an amount equal to about one-fourth of the size of their loans. He also canceled a year's worth of rent, enforced a stricter usury law, and instituted a modern bankruptcy law to provide some measure of protection against aggressive moneylenders.[7]

Caesar additionally enacted a series of minor and probably ineffectual reforms whose purpose seemed solely to curry popular support in his battle against the aristocracy. He brought back laws prohibiting expensive clothing and food, actually sending out soldiers to take away all such items they would find; he required all owners of farmland to employ one free laborer for every two slaves; and he placed a rather low limit on the amount of currency that could be held by any one individual.[8] It was not difficult for anyone to see the general trend of Caesar's reforms, and there is some evidence that Caesar had even more extensive plans for 44 B.C.[9]

Not surprisingly, Caesar's acts aroused great animosity. In 50 B.C., Cicero, already seeing the trend, worried that Caesar's triumph would result in the "plundering [of] the rich".[10] And in *De officiis* (*On duties*), written in 44 B.C., after Caesar's death, Cicero summed up the complaint against Caesar: "Now there are many—and especially those who are ambitious for eminence and glory—who rob one to enrich another; and they expect to be thought generous to their friends, if they put them

[6] M. W. Frederickson, "Caesar, Cicero and the Problem of Debt", *Journal of Roman Studies* 36 (1966): 141.

[7] Ibid., pp. 133–34.

[8] John Dickinson, *Death of a Republic* (New York: Macmillan, 1963), pp. 332–35.

[9] Martin Goodman, *The Roman World: 44 BC–AD 180* (London: Routledge, 1997), p. 30.

[10] Cicero, *Letters to Atticus*, trans. D. R. Shackleton Bailey, Loeb Classical Library 8 (Cambridge: Harvard University Press, 1999), 7.7.7.

in the way of getting rich, no matter by what means."[11] Later in the same work, Cicero wrote plaintively of the injustice inherent in populist "justice":

> And this is the highest statesmanship and the soundest wisdom on the part of a good citizen, not to divide the interests of the citizens but to unite all on the basis of impartial justice. "Let them live in their neighbor's house rent-free." Why so? In order that, when I have bought, built, kept up, and spent my money upon a place, you may without my consent enjoy what belongs to me? What else is that but to rob one man of what belongs to him and to give to another what does not belong to him? And what is the meaning of an abolition of debts, except that you buy a farm with my money; that you have the farm, and I have not my money?[12]

By 44 B.C., the stage was set for the culmination of the conflict between Caesar and the senators who opposed him.[13]

This background brings an assortment of odd features in *Julius Caesar* into focus. Let us begin with the start of the play because, as W. H. Auden noted, "First things in Shakespeare are always important."[14] None of the characters in the opening scene ever appear again in the play. So what is the purpose of beginning this way? It is to highlight the conflict between the *populares* and the *optimates*, between the commoners who are ready to "see Caesar, and to rejoice in his triumph" (1.1.32–33)[15]

---

[11] Cicero, *De officiis*, trans. Walter Miller, Loeb Classical Library 30 (New York: Macmillan, 1913), 1.43.

[12] Ibid., 2.83–84.

[13] Michael Parenti's explanation of the assassination of Caesar (*The Assassination of Julius Caesar* [New York: W. W. Norton, 2003]) nicely illustrates the sharpness of this conflict. In Parenti's telling, Caesar is the latest in a line of bold heroes standing up for the poor, while the senators, most particularly Cicero, are the evil reactionary forces. One need not agree with Parenti's Marxist undertones in order to find the book a lively exploration of this conflict in Rome.

[14] W. H. Auden, *Lectures on Shakespeare*, ed. Arthur Kirsch (Princeton: Princeton University Press, 2000), p. 126.

[15] All quotations from *Julius Caesar* are from the edition published by Ignatius Press: *Julius Caesar*, ed. Joseph Pearce, Ignatius Critical Editions (San Francisco: Ignatius Press, 2012).

and those who are displeased about his rise to power. The two tribunes, Flavius and Marullus, leave the scene preparing to disperse the crowds celebrating Caesar's triumphs and planning to remove all ornaments being placed on monuments to him. We never meet these two again in the play but they are mentioned by Casca when he is relating the story of how Caesar refused the crown: "I could tell you more news too: Marullus and Flavius, for pulling scarfs off Caesar's images, are put to silence" (1.2.283–85). What does this mean? Shakespeare does not elaborate, but Plutarch tells us that Caesar was so incensed at the actions of these two that he stripped them of their offices.[16]

Thus by the end of the first scene we know that there is a conflict in Rome surrounding the figure of Caesar, that on the one side are the commoners and on the other government officials. But with which side are we meant to sympathize? Is Caesar going to be a hero or a villain in this play? It looks like Shakespeare will immediately tell us this in the next scene, which begins with Caesar calling for his wife. The normal expectation at this point would be that Caesar's character will be revealed and we will determine his role within the play that bears his name. But it is a bit surprising to discover that rather than showing where Shakespeare's play stands on the conflict, the scene simply has Caesar ask Antony to touch Calphurnia during the festival of Lupercal, a touch that was popularly believed to cure barrenness. Caesar is then warned about the ides of March, after which he leaves the stage. Note how cleverly Shakespeare leaves the question of whether Caesar is meant to be the hero or the villain hanging in the mind of the audience. Caesar reenters the scene later, only to tell us that he is wary of Cassius, whom we have just heard conspiring. Caesar then disappears from the play until the day of his death.

---

[16] Plutarch, "Life of Julius Caesar", in *The Lives of the Noble Grecians and Romans*, trans. Thomas North (Hertfordshire: Wordsworth, 1998), p. 522. The Thomas North translation of Plutarch's *Lives*, used here, was Shakespeare's primary source of information about the death of Caesar.

Most of what we know about Shakespeare's Caesar we thus can learn only by hearing how the other characters in the play talk about him. Caesar demonstrates very little about himself, and what we do learn about him is rather ambiguous. We certainly know that he is officious, that he speaks about himself in the third person, and that he is very concerned with appearances. We also learn of his quite human frailties. But in the play, Caesar never says a word about the matters that we know were angering a portion of the aristocracy. He never says a word that indicates whether he is ambitious for his own sake or whether he is merely trying to do what is best for the republic.

That the conspirators believe he is ambitious, that he is seeking to become a tyrant, is obvious, but Shakespeare, again quite cleverly, never gives us the ability to evaluate these charges. The crucial moment in which Antony offers the crown to Caesar takes place offstage. When Caesar reenters afterward, Brutus notes that he looks angry, yet Caesar is speaking about his distrust of Cassius and not about the offer of the crown. We hear that he was upset about the crowd's negative reaction to the idea of his being king only through the eyewitness testimony of Casca, about whom Brutus immediately says, "What a blunt fellow is this grown to be! / He was quick mettle when he went to school" (1.2.294–95). And to make sure that we do not miss Casca's dullness of wit, Shakespeare has him note that Cicero offered a telling remark at Caesar's refusal of the crown, a remark that would presumably have made Caesar's motives clear, but alas, the remark was in Greek, and of course Casca knows no Greek. Are we meant to think that Casca is a credible eyewitness or a dullard who cannot understand what he is seeing? Once again, Shakespeare has given little indication of whether or not we are supposed to approve of Caesar's death.

What of the conspirators? Their stated motives, as articulated by their cries throughout the street after the assassination, are clear:

> *Cinna.* Liberty! Freedom! Tyranny is dead!
>   Run hence, proclaim, cry it about the streets.

Cassius. Some to the common pulpits, and cry out
"Liberty, freedom and enfranchisement!" (3.1.78–81)

While the play itself does not dwell on the crimes of Caesar, Cinna declares that his death is ending the reign of tyranny. But whose liberty was being impinged upon by Caesar? Who was being disenfranchised by his actions? While the patricians send that cry out through the streets, the plebeians saw no reduction of liberty during Caesar's reign; they saw no limitation of their rights. Indeed, recalling the opening scene of the play, the plebeians rejoiced in Caesar's triumphs.

Were the conspirators really all that noble, fighting against a tyrannical monster in the name of liberty? Consider Cassius. That he has a deep-seated hatred of Caesar is obvious. But why does he hate Caesar so much? Were Cassius and, by extension, the other conspirators simply motivated by greed? Plutarch is of mixed mind on the matter. On the one hand, he writes that "Cassius even from his cradle could not abide any manner of tyrants . . . ."[17] Yet later he tells us that Cassius was "a hot, choleric, and cruel man, that would oftentimes be carried away from justice for gain, it was certainly thought that he made war, and put himself into sundry dangers, more to have absolute power and authority, than to defend the liberty of his country."[18]

So, is Cassius motivated by hatred of tyranny and love of liberty or by greed and a desire for power to satisfy his lust for gain? On this point, Shakespeare leaves no doubt. In Act 4, we see the conspirators for the first time after the death of Caesar. We discover that Brutus is unhappy with Cassius, and when they meet, they quarrel publicly. Brutus suggests that they should move somewhere more private, and as soon as they are alone, we discover their motives. Cassius is angry with Brutus:

[17] Ibid.
[18] Ibid., pp. 838–39.

That you have wrong'd me doth appear in this:
You have condemn'd and noted Lucius Pella
For taking bribes here of the Sardians;
Wherein my letters, praying on his side,
Because I knew the man, was slighted off.

(4.3.1–5)

Brutus, recognizing the true nature of Cassius' complaint, responds:

Let me tell you, Cassius, you yourself
Are much condemn'd to have an itching palm,
To sell and mart your offices for gold
To undeservers.

(4.3.9–12)

After his portraying of himself as a noble fighter for justice, we discover that Cassius is immersed in bribery, seeking to defend those extorting bribes from others. The hypocritical nature of the conspiracy against Caesar has already become apparent to Brutus:

Remember March, the ides of March remember:
Did not great Julius bleed for justice sake?
What villain touch'd his body, that did stab,
And not for justice? What, shall one of us,
That struck the foremost man of all this world
But for supporting robbers, shall we now
Contaminate our fingers with base bribes,
And sell the mighty space of our large honours
For so much trash as may be grasped thus?
I had rather be a dog and bay the moon
Than such a Roman.

(4.3.18–28)

Note that Brutus is charging Caesar with being a robber for stealing the property of others. It was ostensibly for that reason that the conspiracy formed against Caesar. Yet those same conspirators are now robbing others. Perhaps Caesar was not killed for noble motives after all.

There is a hint of the self-serving motives of the conspirators earlier in the play. Although Cassius, in conversation with others, constantly emphasizes the nature of Caesar's potential for tyranny, he shows his true motives during the one brief moment that he is alone on the stage, his words out of the earshot of others:

> Well, Brutus, thou art noble; yet, I see,
> Thy honorable mettle may be wrought
> From that it is dispos'd. Therefore it is meet
> That noble minds keep ever with their likes;
> For who so firm that cannot be seduc'd?
> Caesar doth bear me hard; but he loves Brutus.
> If I were Brutus now and he were Cassius,
> He should not humour me.
>
> (1.2.307–14)

Cassius is fully aware that the assassination of Caesar was not motivated by a sense of justice, confessing as much in the final moments before his own death: "Caesar, thou are reveng'd, / Even with the sword that kill'd thee" (5.3.45–46). The use of the word "reveng'd" is telling; one can get revenge only for a wrong suffered, not for something that was deserved. Cassius knows that the murder of Caesar was wrong.

Seen this way, it is hard to spin the conspirators as the noble heroes of the play. But what about Caesar's ultimate defenders? Antony begins by looking like the heir to Caesar's attitude toward the poor. After Caesar's death, in the magnificent funeral oratory, he unites his cause with that of the plebeians. As Allan Bloom has noted, "Antony's appeal is based solely on Caesar's benefactions to the people. Caesar could not be a criminal, for he loved the people; that is the sum of Antony's argument." [19] In the funeral scene, Antony makes a big show

[19] Allan Bloom, *Shakespeare's Politics* (Chicago: University of Chicago Press, 1964), p. 83.

of the discovery and the reading of Caesar's will. We discover that the will not only bequeaths seventy-five drachmas to every Roman citizen but also leaves much of Caesar's private estate as common property for the use of all Romans (3.2.242–52). Moreover, Shakespeare further cements our view of Antony as one who has joined with the plebeians against the patricians when Antony declares to the people, "You are not wood, you are not stones, but men" (3.2.142). This is a direct refutation of Marullus' exclamation to the workers in Act 1, scene 1, "You blocks, you stones, you worse than senseless things!" (1.1.36).

So, by the end of Act 3, Shakespeare has left us with no doubt as to where Antony stands in the battle between Caesar and the aristocracy. It would appear that we have finally found the hero of our play. Unlike the conspirators, Antony is standing with the commoners, celebrating with them in an act of great munificence. But we find a very different Antony in Act 4:

> But, Lepidus, go you to Caesar's house;
> Fetch the will hither, and we shall determine
> How to cut off some charge in legacies.
>
> (4.1.7–9)

This line comes as a shock after the rhetoric of Act 3. Far from admiring Caesar's gift to the commoners, Antony wants to find some way to change the terms of the will. The rhetoric of Act 3 is therefore exposed as being empty; it was purely for show. To make sure we do not miss the point, Shakespeare put only two conversations in Act 4: the one in which Antony seeks to change the terms of the will for his own profit and, beginning in the next scene, the one in which we find Cassius similarly exposed as being corrupt.

Antony's financial gain from Caesar's death was not Shakespeare's invention. Cicero directly charged Antony with such:

> You took a vast load of debt off your shoulders at the Temple of Ops [where Caesar had stored a large amount of treasure].

You used the same records to squander more money than is able to be counted. So many things have been transferred from Caesar's house to yours; and there a most lucrative factory of false memoranda and handwritten documents is in operation, and a scandalous market in lands, towns, exemptions, revenues. After all, what but Caesar's death could have relieved your poverty and debt?[20]

In the end, Cassius and Antony look remarkably similar; they are participating in a power play after Caesar's death to see who will get the larger share of the spoils of the state. They differ less in their aims but more in their disposition. Cassius is worried and insecure; Antony is bold and confident. We find Cassius worried about Antony in the early stages of the conspiracy:

> I think it is not meet
> Mark Antony, so well belov'd of Caesar,
> Should outlive Caesar. We shall find of him
> A shrewd contriver; and you know his means,
> If he improve them, may well stretch so far
> As to annoy us all; which to prevent,
> Let Antony and Caesar fall together.
>   (2.1.155–61)

If the aim of Caesar's death was ending the tyranny of Caesar himself, then it would be impossible for Antony to thwart the conspirators after Caesar's death, and thus there is no need to fear Antony's shrewd contriving. Cassius is worried that Antony is a rival. He does not oppose him for any lofty reasons related to liberty, justice, or the end of tyranny; he is merely afraid of a rival in the quest to divide the wealth of Rome.

Antony is deliberate and poised throughout. He joins a hastily formed triumvirate at the beginning of Act 4 but almost immediately seeks to shrink the division of power by a third. For Antony, Lepidus is merely there to help consolidate the

---

[20] Cicero, *Philippics*, trans. D. R. Shackleton Bailey, Loeb Classical Library 189 (Cambridge: Harvard University Press, 2009), 2.35–36.

wealth of Rome for Antony's benefit and to deflect the blame
for such action:

> And though we lay these honours on this man,
> To ease ourselves of divers sland'rous loads,
> He shall but bear them as the ass bears gold,
> The groan and sweat under the business,
> Either led or driven as we point the way;
> And having brought our treasure where we will,
> Then take we down his load, and turn him off,
> Like to the empty ass, to shake his ears
> And graze in commons.

> (4.1.19–27)

Once the number of recipients of wealth and power has been
reduced to two, it does not take long for the split to occur
between Antony and Octavius (5.1.16–20), which will be more
fully explored in Shakespeare's later play, *Antony and Cleopatra*. As we discover in the later play, while Antony has no
trouble beating the conspirators against Caesar, he has met
his match in Octavius.

Both sides in the dispute surrounding Caesar's death are con-
niving, greedy, and self-serving. As Wayne Rebhorn has noted,
by the time of Caesar's death, heroism "no longer means the
service to the 'patria' for which 'pius Aeneas' was known. . . .
Rather, heroism has degenerated into competition *within* the
patria, as the members of the ruling class jockey for positions
of dominance over their fellows."[21] Was there, then, nobody
acting in a noble fashion? It is at this point that Brutus' character shines through the play. While Brutus and Cassius seem
at first glance to be on the same side of the conflict in the
play, the true conflict is between Cassius, Antony, and the rest
of the Roman elite on the one side and Brutus on the other.

Brutus is a reluctant conspirator; it takes Cassius' decep-
tions to convince him to act at all. He has no personal reason

---

[21] Wayne Rebhorn, "The Crisis of the Aristocracy in *Julius Caesar*", *Renaissance Quarterly* 43 (1990): 84.

to oppose Caesar ("I know no personal cause to spurn at him" [2.1.11]) but is convinced that there is a problem on the horizon.

> And since the quarrel
> Will bear no colour for the thing he is,
> Fashion it thus—that what he is, augmented,
> Would run to these and these extremities;
> And therefore think him as a serpent's egg,
> Which, hatch'd, would as his kind grow mischievous,
> And kill him in the shell.
>
> (2.1.28–34)

While the other conspirators are motivated by anger over what Caesar had already done, Brutus is worried about Caesar's possible future actions.

Given that Brutus is explicitly stating that there is nothing that Caesar has yet done that would merit assassination, what are his fears concerning Caesar's possible actions in the future? What are the things that Brutus worries will become "augmented" and "run to these and these extremities"? In Brutus' mind, the conspirators "struck the foremost man of all this world/But for supporting robbers" (4.3.22–23). Brutus acknowledges that Caesar's past actions were simply a form of robbery. Augmented, Brutus can tell in what direction Caesar's history suggests Caesar's future course would lie. Caesar had no right to take the property of others. And that is why, after the assassination, Brutus is quite troubled by the conspirators' actions:

> For I can raise no money by vile means.
> By heaven, I had rather coin my heart,
> And drop my blood for drachmas, than to wring
> From the hard hands of peasants their vile trash
> By any indirection.
>
> (4.3.71–75)

Brutus opposed Caesar for trampling on the liberty of the nobility by robbing them of their property, but he also refuses to steal the property of the commoners. He seems unconcerned with the benefits to his own person and more concerned with the welfare of the polity as a whole.

After Brutus' defeat at Philippi, liberty, the freedom to protect one's property from rulers who would take it, gradually dies. The Roman Republic slips into an empire, headed by a series of rulers who see the world as their own personal playground. In the language of economists, the government becomes nothing other than a rent seeker, an institution in which the officials' primary aim is to extract wealth from the population.[22] Brutus is thus the tragic figure in the play, doing "incalculable harm from the best possible motives".[23] He not only was the "noblest Roman of them all" (5.5.68), but he is the *only* noble Roman in the play. He cares only for the "common good to all" (5.5.72) but loses everything for which he had aimed. Afraid of a tyrant who would rob wealth from the nobility, his actions turn the state over to a set of rulers who would steal wealth from all sections of the population.

Bibliography

Addison, Joseph. *Cato: A Tragedy and Selected Essays*. Edited by Christine Dunn Henderson and Mark E. Yellin. Indianapolis: Liberty Fund, 2004.

Auden, W. H. *Lectures on Shakespeare*. Edited by Arthur Kirsch. Princeton: Princeton University Press, 2000.

Bloom, Allan. *Shakespeare's Politics*. Chicago: University of Chicago Press, 1964.

Cicero. *De officiis*. Translated by Walter Miller. Loeb Classical Library 30. New York: Macmillan, 1913.

———. *Letters to Atticus*. Translated by D. R. Shackleton Bailey. Loeb Classical Library 8. Cambridge: Harvard University Press, 1999.

[22] See, for example, Charles DeLorme Jr., Stacey Isom, and David Kamerschen, "Rent Seeking and Taxation in the Ancient Roman Empire", *Applied Economics* 37 (2005): 705–11.

[23] W. Warde Fowler, *Roman Essays and Interpretations* (Oxford: Clarendon, 1920), p. 279.

————. *Philippics*. Translated by D. R. Shackleton Bailey. Loeb Classical Library 189. Cambridge: Harvard University Press, 2009.

Dante Alighieri. *Inferno*. Translated by Robert and Jean Hollander. New York: Doubleday, 2000.

DeLorme, Charles, Jr., Stacey Isom, and David Kamerschen. "Rent Seeking and Taxation in the Ancient Roman Empire". *Applied Economics* 37 (2005): 705–11.

Dickinson, John. *Death of a Republic*. New York: Macmillan, 1963.

Fowler, W. Warde. *Roman Essays and Interpretations*. Oxford: Clarendon, 1920.

Frederickson, M. W. "Caesar, Cicero and the Problem of Debt". *Journal of Roman Studies* 36 (1966): 128–41.

Goodman, Martin. *The Roman World: 44 BC–AD 180*. London: Routledge, 1997.

Grant, Michael. *Julius Caesar*. New York: McGraw Hill, 1969.

Parenti, Michael. *The Assassination of Julius Caesar*. New York: W. W. Norton, 2003.

Plutarch. *The Lives of the Noble Grecians and Romans*. Translated by Thomas North. Hertfordshire: Wordsworth, 1998.

Rebhorn, Wayne. "The Crisis of the Aristocracy in *Julius Caesar*". *Renaissance Quarterly* 43 (1990): 75–111.

Shakespeare, William. *Coriolanus*. Edited by Tom Crawford Mineola, New York: Dover, 2003.

————. *Julius Caesar*. Edited by Joseph Pearce. Ignatius Critical Editions. San Francisco: Ignatius Press, 2012.

Temin, Peter. "The Economy of the Early Roman Empire". *Journal of Economic Perspectives* 21 (2006), 133–51.

Brutus in Hell

Sophia Mason

As the hapless pilgrim Dante descends further and further into the depths of his inferno, he finds that its raging fires burn cold. Fire and the heat of fires are appropriate symbols for love and love's perversion, lust; but for the hate that Hell truly is, there is no better symbol than ice. When at last Dante and Virgil his guide enter the heart of Hell, they find Satan "standing in the ice up to his chest".

> From every mouth he slashed a sinner
> With his teeth, as if they were a hackle,
> Thus keeping three suffering at a time.
>
> .   .   .   .
> "That soul up there in greatest torment, who has   .
> His head inside and outside shakes his legs,"
> My master [Virgil] said, "is Judas Iscariot.
> Of the other two, who have their heads below,
> The one swinging from the black face is Brutus;
> Look how he twists and turns and yet says nothing.
> The other is Cassius, of sturdy limb.
> But night is coming up again; the time
> Has come to leave. We have seen all there is."[1]

The three coolest seats in Hell are reserved for the three greatest traitors—indeed, the whole ninth circle of ice is devoted to their kind, because treachery is of all sins the coolest, most calculated offense against charity. No one would doubt that Judas "Better-for-Him-That-He-Had-Never-Been-Born" Iscariot belongs in that circle. On the other hand, there

---

[1] Dante Alighieri, *Inferno*, trans. Louis Biancolli (New York: Washington Square Press, 1966), canto 34, p. 140.

173

have always been a great many people who doubt whether Brutus ought to be in it. This is due in large part to William Shakespeare.

The Brutus of Shakespeare (like the Brutus of Plutarch) is something of a hero—a misguided hero, perhaps, but a hero nonetheless, who risks and ultimately loses everything for the sake of his country's freedom. His mission fails, but his heroism lives on. Or does it? Say what you will about Brutus' patriotism, the defining act of his career did not have the effect that he desired. And say what you will about the nobility of Brutus' goals—could anything justify an act of betrayal such as he commits?

When Brutus first appears in the play, he fears that Caesar may become a tyrant; but his reasons for fearing are very different from Cassius'. Cassius is envious of Caesar, while Brutus is jealous for Rome. Cassius himself recognizes this difference of motive. He speaks of honor before Brutus, who "love[s]/ The name of honour more than [he] fear[s] death" (1.2.88–89),[2] but acknowledges privately that the deed they are contemplating is dishonorable: "Well, Brutus, thou art noble; yet, I see,/Thy honourable mettle may be wrought/From that it is dispos'd" (1.2.307–9). Brutus is too noble a man to respond to Cassius' flatteries; but it is that very nobility, that "honourable mettle" of Brutus', which brings him into a dishonorable conspiracy against his friend Caesar.

The conspirators want Brutus to join them precisely because of this virtue. He "sits high in all the people's hearts", and his countenance will change the offense of Caesar's murder "to virtue and to worthiness" in their eyes (1.3.157, 160). The final word on him comes from Mark Antony, who, after speaking truth about Brutus (albeit deceptively) in the funeral oration, concludes the play by declaring him "the noblest Roman of them all".

---

[2] All quotations from *Julius Caesar* are from the edition published by Ignatius Press: *Julius Caesar*, ed. Joseph Pearce, Ignatius Critical Editions (San Francisco: Ignatius Press, 2012).

All the conspirators save only he
Did that they did in envy of great Caesar;
He only in a general honest thought
And common good to all made one of them.
(5.5.68–72)

Brutus' motivation is supposed, even by his enemies, to be pure; and in the abstract his action does seem to be just: in the hopes of preserving a better form of government, he slew a man whom he thought would become a tyrant.

It must be by his death; and for my part,
I know no personal cause to spurn at him,
But for the general: he would be crown'd.
How that might change his nature, there's the question.
It is the bright day that brings forth the adder,
And that craves wary walking. Crown him—that!
And then, I grant, we put a sting in him . . . .
(2.1.10–16)

But is Brutus correct in supposing that Caesar will misuse his power? And even if he supposes rightly, is he justified in killing his friend to save the state? Even if he is justified, will Roman freedom be preserved by the assassination?

The answer to the last question seems almost certainly to be no. The Roman people are ruled by the Senate and the tribunes, and they might be ruled by Caesar; but they are incapable of governing themselves. In the first scene of the play, we see how easily they are swayed. The supreme demonstration of their malleability comes in the scene immediately following Caesar's death, where they are led in a mere quarter of an hour from wishing Brutus crowned to wishing Brutus dead. They are sheep—not very nice or intelligent sheep either. If Brutus thought he was preserving any form of self-government for the people, he was mistaken. It could even be argued that a firm hand like Caesar's might do the people good. The graver objection to Brutus' part in the enterprise, the one that led Dante to consign him to the black mouth of

Satan, is his breaking of trust with Caesar. Mark Antony—
ever adept at seeing the truth, if also at taking liberties with—
calls Brutus "Caesar's angel" (3.2.181). How inconceivable to
Caesar that his angel should fall! When, too late, it becomes
apparent to Caesar that Brutus is one of his assassins ("Et tu,
Brute?" [3.1.77]), *then* he dies. If the angelic Brutus is cor-
ruptible, Caesar might as well give up his life; if Brutus can
fall, Caesar can fall. Nor is Caesar merely mistaken in Brutus'
affection, any more than he is mistaken about Cassius' "lean
and hungry" look (1.2.194). Brutus does love Caesar, but "[he]
lov[es] Rome more" (3.2.23).[3]

In the pre-Christian world of *Julius Caesar*, Brutus' action
is the ultimate, the paradigmatic, betrayal of friendship. Perhaps if Brutus had challenged Caesar openly, it would not
have been so. If Brutus had retired from Rome, informed
Caesar that he could no longer take part in the destruction
of the Roman polity—if he had given "fair warning"—
then it is doubtful that his opposition to Caesar would be
open to the charge of treachery. (It is equally doubtful that
it would have been successful, though that is another matter.) As it is, Brutus gives no sign to Caesar that he considers
their friendship at an end, drops no hints of dissatisfaction
with Caesar's behavior, but determines to do what is "not an
office for a friend" without warning (5.5.29)—and so breaks
the friendship off in the most brutal and complete manner
possible.

What makes his action all the more regrettable is the possible absence of necessity for it. Caesar is unquestionably
arrogant—

---

[3] See also 1.2.78–82 ("Brutus: 'What means this shouting? I do fear the people/
Choose Caesar for their king.'/ Cassius: 'Aye, do you fear it?/Then I must
think you would not have it so.'/Brutus: 'I would not, Cassius; *yet I love him
well.*'" [emph. added]) and 3.1.183 ("... I ... did love Caesar when I struck
him"). Most interesting are Cassius' accusatory lines in the middle of his quarrel with Brutus: "Strike as thou didst at Caesar; for I know,/When thou didst
hate him worst, thou lov'dst him better/Than ever thou lov'dst Cassius"
(4.3.104–6).

I could be well mov'd, if I were as you . . . .

. . . .

But I am constant as the northern star . . . .

. . . .

The skies are painted with unnumb'red sparks,
They are all fire, and every one doth shine;
But there's but one in all doth hold his place.
So in the world: 'tis furnish'd well with men,
And men are flesh and blood, and apprehensive;
Yet in the number I do know but one
That unassailable holds on his rank,
Unshak'd of motion; and . . . I am he . . . .

(3.1.58, 60, 63–70)

—and he certainly wants to be king—

> [T]hen he [Antony] offered [the crown] to him again; then he
> put it by again; but to my thinking, he was very loath to lay
> his fingers off it. . . . Marry, before he fell down, when he
> perceiv'd the common herd was glad he refus'd the crown, he
> pluckt me ope his doublet, and offer'd them his throat to cut.
> (1.2.240ff., 262ff.)

—but this is not to say that he would make a *bad* king. (*Pace*
Roman republicanism, not every king is a Tarquin.) In fact,
given Caesar's love and admiration for Brutus, it is quite possible that Caesar shares some of Brutus' nobility and even some
of his patriotism; certainly Brutus might have influenced Caesar
for the good if the latter had been crowned. It is an interesting exercise to wonder how Roman history might have looked
if Brutus had tried a subtler approach to politics.

But Brutus cannot see Caesar the man for Caesar the
would-be king. Brutus' Stoicism[4] has led him to treat Caesar

---

[4] See especially Brutus' exchange with Portia in 2.1; his quarrel with Cassius
in 4.3, particularly Brutus' lines 105–12, ("sheathe your dagger" through "straight
is cold again") and Cassius' lines near 150 (Brutus' line "Portia is dead" through
Cassius' response "How scaped I killing when I crossed you so?"); and Brutus'
reflections on Cato's suicide and the Stoic attitude toward death at 5.1.100–18

not as a man who might be influenced, nor even as a friend to whom his loyalty is owed, but almost as the form of the tyrant—a spirit, and an evil one.

This Stoicism of Brutus' is both his great virtue and his downfall. He has a passion for being dispassionate, an attachment to being detached. His selflessness makes him proof against Cassius' flattery, but it also blinds him to the proper affections, and consequently the proper behavior, that should exist between him and his wife and him and his friends. Selflessness may imply a willingness to die for a cause, and that selflessness Brutus certainly has. The selflessness that he lacks—that every Christian must recognize—is that which makes a man willing to die for his friend. This is the real difference between the Christian and the pagan. The Christian's heroism is personal; the pagan's is impersonal.

Brutus is not easy throwing away Caesar's life—"O that we then could come by Caesar's spirit, / And not dismember Caesar!" (2.1.169–70)—but this wish is not more than a wish, and his resolution to assassinate Caesar remains unchanged. The great irony of the assassination is that Caesar's spirit lives and visits the murderers at Philippi; metaphorically, the tyrannic spirit that Brutus wished to destroy was unleashed by Caesar's death, which led to the rise of the triumvirate and subsequently to imperial Rome.

Brutus could not have foreseen all this—yet there are some things surely that he should have foreseen and that he should be blamed for not having foreseen. He is so accustomed to the Stoic disregard—indeed, the Stoic disdain—for emotion, affection, desire, greed, and the myriad things that make men human, that he makes a poor judge of those around him. His wife Portia, easily the most loyal person in the play, is initially excluded from the conspiracy in part because of his mistrust of her. He overrates the Roman spirit and underrates Caesar's affection for himself. He goes against Cassius' warning and lets

("Even by the rule of that philosophy" through "If not, why then this parting was well made").

Mark Antony speak over Caesar's body ("You know not what you do. Do not consent/That Antony speak in his funeral" [3.1.233–34])—and does not even stick around to hear what is said or to have the last word! His joining with Cassius in the conspiracy is particularly ill judged. How *can* Brutus suppose that slaying Caesar will free Rome when Caesar II (who is, like most sequels, a corrupt parody of the original) is right behind him? Brutus must either presume that Cassius is as honorable as he (sheer idiocy, given Cassius' words in their first scene together) or assume for some reason that Cassius' greed will not matter in the end—which is idiocy of another, profounder sort.

Brutus' Stoicism leads to his renown and to his downfall—a downfall that is both temporal and, according to Dante, eternal. But somewhere along the road to Philippi there is a change in him. He will not mourn the death of his wife; but he shows his servant affection. He does not repent the death of Caesar; but he is visited by Caesar's ghost. He cannot make peace with the ghost; but he weeps over the death of Cassius ("Friends, I owe moe tears/To this dead man than you shall see me pay" [5.3.101–2]). It is a strange thing that he would not spare the man he loved but should be so moved by the death of a man whom he had come at moments almost to hate—a strange thing, but the tears for Cassius are there. To forgive Cassius is mere Stoicism, but to weep for him is a kind of affection, and affection may be a kind of charity. If there is hope for Brutus' soul, it lies not in his patriotism but in his tears.

The Renaissances of G. J. Caesar and M. J. Brutus

Susan Vandiver Nicassio
University of Louisiana at Lafayette

This was the noblest Roman of them all.
All the conspirators save only he
Did that they did in envy of great Caesar;
He only in a general honest thought
And common good to all made one of them.
His life was gentle; and the elements
So mix'd in him that Nature might stand up
And say to all the world, "This was a man!"
— Shakespeare, *Julius Caesar* (1599), 5.5.68–75[1]

For all these reasons I can sooner claim to have freed Florence—
having left her without a tyrant—than they [his Florentine crit-
ics] can claim that I have done something wrong.
— Lorenzino "Lorinzaccio" de'Medici,
Apologia (1539)[2]

It is a great presumption to kill the ruler of a public administra-
tion, be he just or unjust, without knowing absolutely what good
will come from his death.... I have become tired of, and unable
to bear, those who say that no good can be done if one does not
begin with an evil, and that is with death.
— Michelangelo, in Giannotti's
Dialogues on . . . Dante (1539)[3]

And those who read ancient history will always recognize this:
after a change of government, whether from a republic to a tyr-

---

[1] All quotations from *Julius Caesar* are from the edition published by Ignatius
Press: *Julius Caesar*, ed. Joseph Pearce, Ignatius Critical Editions (San Francisco:
Ignatius Press, 2012).
[2] Lorenzino de'Medici, *Apology for a Murder*, trans. Andrew Brown (London:
Hesperus Press), p. 18.
[3] Donato Giannotti, *Dialogi di Donato Giannotti, De' giorni che Dante consumò
nel cercare l'Inferno e 'l Purgatorio*, quoted in Piccolomini, *Brutus Revival*, p. 91.

anny or from a tyranny to a republic, there must be a memorable
punishment of those who are the enemies of the present state of
affairs. And so, he who establishes a tyranny and does not kill
Brutus,[4] and he who establishes a democratic regime and does
not kill the sons of Brutus, will not last long.

— Machiavelli, *The Prince* (1513)[5]

"The soul up there whose punishment is worst,"
　　the teacher said, "is Judas Iscariot,
　　whose feet stick out and who is chewed headfirst.
Of the two others with their heads hung down,
　　the one who hangs from the black snout is Brutus.
　　See how he writhes and does not speak a word!
Cassius is last, who looks so squarely built.
　　But night is rising, and it's time to leave,
　　for Hell has nothing more for us to see."

— Dante, *Inferno* (1314)[6]

On one side, we have Caesar: arrogant, aging, superstitious,
growing ever more fond of ceremonial display, and clearly seeing himself as an absolute monarch. But he is the fixed center
that holds together a world only recently emerged from civil
war, a Roman world (in the as-yet-unseen divine plan) des-
tined to be the seedbed for the Christian world.

On the other side, we have Brutus: a Stoic, honest, intelligent, honorable, and a descendant of the Lucius Junius Brutus
who, the ancient story said, established the Roman Republic
and kept it at the cost of condemning his own sons to death.
He is surrounded by conspirators whose motives vary from outrage to ambition to greed. But his aim is to save the republic
from tyranny.

The dilemma: Is it licit to kill Caesar?

[4] The reference is to Lucius Junius Brutus, the ancestor of Marcus Junius Brutus, Caesar's assassin.

[5] Niccolo Machiavelli, *Discourses on Livy*, trans. Henry Neville (London: 1675,
reprinted in 1772), 111:3:1, http://www.constitution.org/mac/disclivy3.htm,
accessed 9/2/2011.

[6] Dante Alighieri, *Inferno*, trans. Anthony Esolen (New York: Modern Library,
2003), 34.61–69.

Ever since that fateful afternoon in mid-March 44 B.C., the killing in Pompey's theater in Rome has echoed down the centuries. Contemporary and later Roman writers considered the event to be the major turning point in Roman history; medieval theologians saw Caesar (inaccurately) as the founder of the empire that facilitated the spread of Christianity; Dante's immortal *Divine Comedy* ends its most widely known segment— the *Inferno*—with an unforgettable image of the punishment of Brutus and Cassius.

But for the modern West, the story of the assassination and its consequences has been transmitted almost exclusively by William Shakespeare, whose *Julius Caesar* has long been the play most assigned in high school classes. The play has this status for a number of reasons: its language is relatively easy for modern English speakers, it offers a view of ancient Rome that is relatively familiar to most, and it offers a rich basis for political and moral debate for those so inclined.

So long as classical education endures, the image of Caesar remains current. It is largely due to Shakespeare that Caesar, like Napoleon, is one of those figures who have (at least until recently) been immediately recognizable by even the most minimally educated. If Bugs Bunny struck a pose with a tricorner hat and his hand to his chest, he was Napoleon; if he wrapped himself in a toga and Elmer Fudd stabbed him, he was Caesar. Ninety-nine percent of the audience could be depended on to get the joke.

The question of the right or wrong in the murder of Caesar is, in fact, the question of whether it is licit or not to take the life of whatever tyrant is currently troubling the peace of the world. One side argues, with Dante, that to kill a ruler, even a dangerous and wicked one, is to act against divine providence, since it is impossible to tell what good or evil will result from the rule, or from the murder, or to foresee what divine plans for ultimate good may be thwarted. Those who believe that tyrannicide is the appropriate response to tyranny argue that to kill a tyrant, even—or especially—at the sacrifice of one's own life, is the greatest possible act of patriotism and virtue.

The dilemma is at root the old question: Can one do evil to bring about good? The question is far from simple and is far from being limited to the formal assassination of rulers. Is it licit to bomb an abortion clinic? Or to detonate an explosive vest in a crowded bus? Or to hurl a Molotov cocktail at an advancing tank? Even those who praise tyrannicide admit that a greater evil, such as civil war, may follow such a deed; and even those who condemn tyrannicide admit that those who commit it can be noble and intensely admirable.

So Michelangelo, a republican at heart, was troubled when he learned of the assassination of Alessandro, the first Medici Duke of Florence. He was tired of the arguments in favor of bloodshed, but he sculpted a bust of Brutus in the killer's honor, a bust that transformed Renaissance portrait sculpture.

Shakespeare, as is his way, takes us to the heart of this dilemma. The nobility and idealism of Brutus result in a deed that brings bloody ruin to the republic and ushers in a tyranny far more effective and drastic than that of Caesar.

Gaius Julius Caesar did indeed "bestride the narrow world/ Like a Colossus", as Cassius puts it in Shakespeare's play (1.2.135–36). If the conspirators hoped to change that by the simple expedient of killing him, they were of course badly mistaken. Assassination only put the seal on his immortality. He became not just a brilliant general and a would-be despot but a touchstone for all debates over political realities, whether they be monarchies, tyrannies, republics, or democracies.

The story of Julius Caesar—his accomplishments, his ambition, and his death—has continually been reinterpreted through the ages, according to changing circumstances. In the late thirteenth and the early fourteenth century, Dante Alighieri saw Caesar as the founder of empire, and empire as the one reliable defense against a world of faction and war. In his *Comedy*, he consigns Brutus and Cassius to the Caina, the circle of the traitors, the deepest pit of Hell.

The men of the Renaissance, poised between quarreling republics and tyranny, looked back to a golden age of Greeks and Romans. They found in Caesar and his assassins an allegory for their own political dilemmas. The republicans of *quattro-cento* Florence had little use for Caesar and glorified Brutus and tyrannicide as the last defense against despotism.

William Shakespeare, rediscovering Plutarch, found there a world as complex and as morally ambiguous as the dying years of the Tudor monarchy. Shakespeare's Caesar is indecisive, vain, superstitious, and a real threat to liberty; Brutus, as Mark Antony hammers home to us, is an "honorable man". But the murder of Caesar lets slip the dogs of war and collapses the empire into bloody chaos. It is indeed tempting to see coded references to the idealists of the Reformation, who, by attacking the authority of a flawed papacy, brought persecution and bloodshed to England.

Dante's Romans

Dante was the devoted disciple of the great Roman political poet, Virgil. He was also a politically active, office-holding citizen of Florence, a city torn between factions (as were many cities of the time): the Ghibbelines, who supported the Holy Roman Emperor's claims for political authority over the Italian states, and the Guelfs, who at least nominally backed the authority of the popes as supreme. Though the quarrels often had little to do with either emperor or pope, the bloodshed, the confiscations, and the sentences of exile and death were very real, as Dante would discover. Exiled in 1303 when his party lost control of the city, he lost his home and family, and perhaps most painful, he lost his homeland, Florence. Wandering about Italy from patron to patron, he determined to reject partisan politics and become a "party of one", placing all of his hope in the return of a Holy Roman Emperor who would pacify and defend Italy.

This is not the place to attempt the impossible task of boiling Dante's *Commedia* (or his *De Monarchia* or *Convivio*) down to a few key points. But it is fair to say that one of the major themes of the *Commedia*, and indeed of Dante's political thinking as a whole, is his conviction that Italy could be saved only by a strong and just secular government. The Holy Roman Empire, he hoped, could recreate the unity and peace of Rome. A good emperor could provide the warring Italian states with the stability they so bitterly lacked and save the Church from the corruption that came with attempting to wield both of the two swords.

De Monarchia, Dante's most overtly political work, concludes that monarchy (such as the Holy Roman Empire) is the natural and most stable and benevolent form of government. He bases this conclusion on a discussion of Roman examples, arguing that Rome was divinely ordained to rule the world at its most critical time, the time of the Incarnation. This divinely ordained empire (which medieval theory supposed to have been founded by Julius Caesar) was to be in no way inferior or superior to the Church. Both were founded by God, each had its own purpose, and both were of equal legitimacy.

In the *Convivio*, written probably around 1307–1308, Dante looks to the teaching of Aristotle that man is a political, or social, animal, drawn to live in community. But for the Christian, man is also a fundamentally flawed creature, given to envy, anger, pride, and all the other deadly sins that make life in community difficult. The Empire, he argues, is the tool ordained by God to control these sinful passions and thereby allow citizens to live in peace and order: "No nation ever was or will be more tempered in the exercise of rule, stronger in preservation and more clever in acquiring it than ... that sacred people in whom was mingled the lofty blood of the Trojans, namely Rome. God chose this people for that office." [7]

Led by Virgil, and hoping for the restoration of Rome, Dante's tour through the afterlife bristles with Greeks and Romans, historical, mythical, and literary. It is striking that in the *Commedia* one meets Lucius Junius Brutus, who overthrew the Tarquins and established the Roman Republic, in the almost

---

[7] Dante Alighieri, *Convivio*, trans. Richard Lansing (London: J. M. Dent, 1903), pp. 156–57.

pleasant fields of Limbo. If the Brutus who expelled the Tarquins is in Limbo, and Caesar's assassins are so prominently punished in the mouth of Satan, we might expect to find Caesar himself, credited by medieval theologians with founding the long-destined empire, richly rewarded, perhaps even among the just rulers in Purgatory or among the handful of pagans who, surprisingly, are found in Paradise. But instead we find him a remote and shadowy figure, glimpsed but not encountered, in Limbo.

Most of Limbo is a place where those who lived before Christ who "did not give God homage as they ought" are "hopeless, ... forever in desire", in a dim forest "thicketed with souls", a place of sorrow but not punishment, filled with "sighs that made a trembling in the everlasting air".[8]

Emerging from the forest, Dante sees a blazing ring of light[9]—a castle in a broad green field, surrounded by a moat and rings of light quelling the darkness. Here are the souls who, like the others, failed to give God the honor owed him. But their glorious deeds on earth have earned them a place in the light that is created by the learning, intellect, and glory of those who dwell there. Here Caesar walks, in a Christian version of the Elysian fields. This is the home of Virgil, Dante's guide and beloved teacher—and also of Homer, Lucan, and others. Walking across the "meadows bright as fine-enameled green",[10] he sees a group of the heroes of Troy and of Rome (Virgil, of course, firmly linked Troy and Rome in his masterpiece, the *Aeneid*). In the distance Dante sees Hector and Aeneas and "Cesare armato con gli occhi grifagni" (in arms, Caesar with his falcon eye).[11] Caesar's daughter Julia is there as well, along with Cato's much-loved wife, Martia.

The group also includes Brutus, the ancestor of Caesar's assassin, who drove out the Etruscan tyrants to become the first

[8] Dante, *Inferno*, 4, 38–42, 26–27, p. 35; 65–56, p. 37.
[9] Ibid., 67–68, p. 37.
[10] Ibid., 4, 118–22, p. 39.
[11] Ibid., 4, 123, p. 39.

consul of republican Rome. This is puzzling. Not only did this
proto-Brutus precipitate a bloody revolution, but he overthrew a legitimate monarch. Worse, he ordered the death of
his own sons when they plotted to return the Etruscan rulers.
Why is he rewarded as a founder of Rome, while his descendant is condemned?

As mentioned above, medieval political theorists believed
that God had from the beginning of time ordained the
Roman Empire as the seedbed of Christianity. Lucius Junius
Brutus' deed moved that plan forward; the deed of Marcus
Junius Brutus was—whether he realized it or not—an attempt
to thwart it.

Renaissance Romans

No Florentine political thinker could overlook Dante, the
iconic Florentine intellectual. But the view of Brutus as the
greatest of sinners was a hard one for them to accept. Brutus—
scholarly, rigorously honest, the epitome of *virtù*—was an attrac-
tive figure for civic humanists, who looked to the classical world
for models. Florence, menaced by authoritarian states like
Milan, ruled by the Visconti, saw itself as the Roman Republic reborn. Brutus, the killer of a tyrant, was a model defender
of the republic. Florence, the intellectually and artistically domi-
nant Renaissance republic, developed a complex republican
ideology based on civic humanism and admiration for the
Greco-Roman tradition that they wanted to recreate. The classical writers all agreed that the central political event of the
Roman world was the assassination of Caesar by Brutus, Cassius, and the other conspirators.

Florentine intellectuals fell back on the idea that Brutus and
Cassius were not placed in Hell as *individuals* but rather as rep-
resentatives of a type. Michelangelo, troubled by the assassination of the first Medici Duke of Florence but approving of
the assassin's aims, put it this way: "[Dante] needed very famous
examples, and could not find any more or equally famous than
Brutus and Cassius; . . . he did not place them in hell as Brutus

and Cassius, but as examples of those who betray Imperial majesty."[12]

Tyrannicide and attempted tyrannicide were in fashion in Renaissance Italy. In the last quarter of the fifteenth century, there were any number of Brutusesque assassinations and assassination attempts; virtually every would-be tyrannicide justified his actions by citing Brutus. In Milan three young nobles murdered Galeazzo Maria Sforza, then tyrant of the city. Under torture Girolamo Olgiati, one of the assassins, compared himself to Brutus, and at his grisly, Renaissance-style public execution, he managed a few eloquently Roman last words: "Mors acerba, fama perpetua, stabit vetua memoria facit" (Death is bitter, fame is eternal—the memory of my deed will endure).

Even more famous was the 1478 Pazzi conspiracy against the Medici in Florence. The Pazzi, a rival banking family, plotted to overthrow the Medici with the help of co-conspirators, who included the Salviati family, the nephew of Pope Sixtus IV (and very likely Sixtus himself), and Federico da Montefeltro, the renowned Duke of Urbino. The aim was to kill Lorenzo de'Medici, "the Magnificent", and his brother, Giuliano. Giuliano died; Lorenzo escaped. Many of the conspirators and suspected conspirators were lynched; those who escaped lynching were executed. One conspirator, Pietro Paolo Boscoli, on the night before his execution, called for his friend Luca della Robbia, and della Robbia left an account of their meeting. Boscoli had gone into the affair convinced that it was a good and noble thing to imitate the actions of Brutus. But, facing death, he realized that he had in fact been a party to murder, a grievous sin. "Then he said, 'Please, Luca, take Brutus out of my head, so that I may go through this totally as a Christian.'"[13]

The oddest, most famous, and clearest example of the Renaissance Caesar-Brutus tradition took place in January 1537 when Alessandro, the first Medici Duke of Florence, was killed by

---

[12] Giannotti, *Dialogi*, p. 85, quoted in Piccolomini, *Brutus Revival*, p. 95.

[13] Franklin L. Ford, *Political Murder: From Tyrannicide to Terrorism* (Cambridge: Harvard University Press, 1985), p. 138, cited in Piccolomini, *Brutus Revival*, p. 76.

his cousin, Lorenzino (little Lorenzo), also called Lorenzaccio (ugly, clumsy, or nasty Lorenzo).

Alessandro, given the title of duke by the Holy Roman Emperor at age nineteen, may or may not have been the illegitimate son of Guilio de'Medici (later Pope Clement VII) and an African servant, and thus a grand-nephew of Lorenzo the Magnificent. He had been placed on the throne by his uncle (some historians say, his father) Pope Clement VII, with the support of the Holy Roman Emperor, after the collapse of the short-lived Florentine republic.[14] The anti-Medici exiles accused him of cruelty and corruption, charges that may or may not have been true. What certainly was true was that his cousin and constant companion Lorenzino was a strange young man, and very possibly a psychopath.

Lorenzino's main claim to fame had been to go on a teenage rampage in Rome, during which he decapitated several ancient imperial statues at the Arch of Constantine. In Florence, he acted as court jester, pimp, and partner in crime to his cousin, the young duke.

In January 1537 Lorenzino lured the duke to the bedroom of Lorenzino's pretty aunt, where the duke expected an evening's entertainment, with or without her willing cooperation. Instead of finding the lady, Alessandro was met by his cousin and a hired tough, who hacked him to death. It was not a glorious or heroic event, and the end result was a new Medici duke, Cosimo I, who would reign for almost forty years and cement Medici control over Florence until the eighteenth century.

Some disgruntled Florentine exiles, supporters of the late republic, briefly hailed Lorenzino as a tyrannicide in the tradition of Brutus. As noted earlier, even Michelangelo, working in Rome, was inspired to sculpt a portrait bust of Brutus in Lorenzino's honor. But the young man's dubious character was too well known for him to attract any real support.

---

[14] This was the ill-fated republic that Machiavelli had served as secretary and for which Michelangelo had helped design the military defenses.

This did not prevent him from having a medal struck to commemorate the assassination. The iconography is unmistakably in the Brutus tradition. During the last battles of the Roman civil war, Brutus had a silver denarius struck to pay his troops and to remind them of why they were fighting. On one side was the bust of Brutus, young, firm of jaw, and unadorned. On the other was a liberty cap, two drawn daggers, and the words EID MAR—the ides of March, a day no one could forget. Lorenzino's medal is clearly a copy, Renaissance style: the young assassin is elegantly draped, bearded and bareheaded, hair brushed forward a la Brutus. On the obverse are the liberty cap and the daggers (in this case, upside down) and the date, VII ID IAN, to commemorate the assassination of Duke Alessandro.

Lorenzino, unlike Brutus, was not a Stoic, or truthful, or honorable. The Florentine republican exiles wanted nothing to do with him, and his *Apologia*, written in defense of his action, was and is generally regarded as a masterpiece of Renaissance rhetoric more or less devoid of truth. Unlike Brutus, he died not a suicide on the battlefield but cut down in a Venetian alley by a thug in the pay of the Medici, on the second Sunday of Lent 1548.

Shakespeare's Romans

The Renaissance came late to the North, but by the late sixteenth century the classical humanism born in Italy had arrived at the courts, schools, and playhouses of Tudor England. A glance at any list of Shakespearean plays shows how many of them were set in Italy or borrowed from Italian sources: *Romeo and Juliet*, *The Merchant of Venice*, *Two Gentlemen of Verona*, *A Midsummer Night's Dream*, and *A Comedy of Errors* are only the most famous of them. In addition to the plays set in Italy or using Italian plots, there were plays—*Julius Caesar* the best known—set in classical times and relying heavily on classical sources.

Scholars agree that Shakespeare's primary classical source for *Julius Caesar* was the new translation of Plutarch by Sir

Thomas North, published in 1579, thirty or so years after Lorenzino's assassination of Alessandro and twenty years before the
play first appeared at the new Globe theater. Unlike Lucan
and Suetonius (sources available to Dante), Plutarch presents
a more nuanced and sympathetic view of the assassins. Shakespeare's presentation of Brutus is even more nuanced and sympathetic than is Plutarch's. This is astonishing, given the
context of the play's first performances.

Julius Caesar was first performed in 1599, four years before
the aging Queen Elizabeth would die. The death of any Renaissance ruler was a dangerous time, but the impending death of
Elizabeth was especially perilous. She left no direct heir, a situation that always opened the door to power struggles and
potential war. Worse, Elizabeth's long reign had put the seal
on three generations of religious persecution and civil unrest.
Since 1535 a political and intellectual elite had inexorably
sought to eradicate Catholicism in England. Whatever its theo-
retical justification, this English "Reformation" certainly led
to more power for the powerful.

Some critics see Shakespeare's Caesar as the representative
of the English monarchy, or even monarchy in the abstract.
Shakespeare's view of the conspirators, and especially of Brutus, is dramatically more favorable than that offered by any of
the ancient sources, including Plutarch. Shakespeare's Caesar,
like Dante's, is curiously remote—he appears only in a few scenes
early in the play and briefly as a ghost later. He is deeply flawed:
superstitious, indecisive, almost ridiculously self-important, and
partial to ceremony; it is only his death that reveals him as the
one man essential for the continuance of civil order.

Brutus, at least (the other conspirators have less pure motives),
is rigorously honest and idealistic. He is struggling to decide
what to do when presented with a friend who now poses a threat
to the republic that Brutus' own (probably mythical) ancestor
had established. A Stoic to the core, not even the horrific suicide of his beloved Portia can shake his demeanor or his resolve.
He is what his enemies proclaim him to be at the end of the
play, "the noblest Roman of them all". But the death of Caesar,

rather than leading to freedom and a renewal of republican virtue, in fact leads to nothing but death, division, and ruin.

It is tempting to look at the play not through a simply political lens (that is, in terms of republicanism versus monarchy)
but rather through one that better suits conditions of Shakespeare's own time and place: a lens of religious strife, in which
an elite group of religious revolutionaries had destroyed an old
governance. They, like the assassins of Caesar, acted with mixed
motives: some absolutely pure, some vengeful. Many were hoping for personal power and profit.

If *Julius Caesar* provides a lens through which to see the
author's present, what did Shakespeare see when he viewed
the ancient past? A nation poised on the brink of civil war,
torn between opposing ideologies: Brutus and the conspirators
determine to remove Caesar, who challenges their ideological
purity and threatens to overthrow the ancient republic. But
his death removed the lynchpin that held the world together,
and lacking that central unifying point, the Roman polis fell
apart into mutually destructive parties and into tyranny.

Is *Julius Caesar* a plea for political unity in the face of a dangerous regime change? Or is it perhaps a warning that the idealists who were so determined to force reformation onto the
Church in England had in the end brought disaster? Is it a plea
for the authority of the pope as the essential unifying force of
Christianity? Or maybe the play is all of the above—and more.

Julius Caesar was by no means the end of the dark romance
of assassination a la Brutus. French revolutionaries and their
admirers copied the Brutus haircut, slightly curled, long at the
back, and brushed forward over the brow. American revolutionaries proclaimed themselves to be Brutuses confronting the
tyranny of George III's Caesar. Patrick Henry, during the debates
over the Stamp Act (1765), is quoted as declaring that "Caesar
had his Brutus, Charles the First his Cromwell, and George III
may profit by their example."[15]

---

[15] Marion Mills Miller, *Great Debates in American History* (New York: Current Literature Publishing Company. 1913), vol. 1, p. 25.

True to the developing tradition of revolutions and civil struggles, American revolutionaries went on to attack one another
as would-be Caesars. John Adams and Thomas Jefferson compared Alexander Hamilton to Caesar, Adams going so far as
to write, "When Burr shot Hamilton it was not Brutus killing
Caesar in the Senate-House, but it was killing him before he
passed the Rubicon." Burr shot back, comparing Jefferson to
"Caesar rejecting the trappings but tenaciously grasping the
substance of imperial domination."[16]

The American debate over history's most famous and most
influential assassination did not end with the American Revolution. Whig attempts to brand Andrew Jackson as another
Caesar were blamed for an assassination attempt on Jackson
himself. John Wilkes Booth, the "American Brutus", cried out
"Sic semper tyrannis" after he killed his Caesar, Abraham
Lincoln.[17]

In the aftermath of World War II, when the United States
was triumphantly wrapping itself in the trappings of popular
democracy, a popular radio series—*You Are There!*—offered its
own breaking-news-style presentation of the events of the ides
of March 44 B.C.[18] In it, Caesar turns out to have been a populist democrat whose empowerment of the "Roman in the street"
drove the oligarchy to murder him.

The echoes of the confrontation between Caesar and Brutus, autocracy and republic, tyrant and liberator, reform and
conservative—call it what you will—continue. From Dante
to Shakespeare to the American Revolution to the twentieth-
century world wars, the tragedy of Caesar and Brutus remains,
and is likely to remain, part of the Western psyche so long as
tyrants and patriots exist—or at least until classical education
and historical knowledge disappear altogether.

---

[16] Carl Richard, *Twelve Greeks and Romans Who Changed the World* (Lanham,
Maryland: Rowman and Littlefield, 2003), p. 176.

[17] Michael W. Kauffman, *American Brutus: John Wilkes Booth and the Lincoln
Conspiracies* (New York: Random House, 2004). The actor-assassin's father was
named Junius Brutus Booth.

[18] "The Assassination of Caesar", broadcast March 8, 1953.

Cassius and the Tragedy of Rome

Andrew T. Seeley
Thomas Aquinas College

We can imagine that Shakespeare's London, the center of enormous political, religious, and social turmoil, a leading capital city on the edge of modernity, was filled with an enormous variety of human characters from every social class. Shakespeare was uniquely positioned to experience them all—and uniquely gifted to take them all into his stories and make the most of them. For a political play like *Julius Caesar*, driven as it is by the interaction of leading men in an unsettled time, Shakespeare drew upon his experience to present many different types of characters, each acting and reacting to the dawn of a new order in different ways.

In unsettled times, the decisions of the men who stand out among the crowd matter more than ever. The tried and true ways, the systematic workings of law and bureaucracy, election and review, no longer provide a sufficient channel for the enormous human energies of a great people. Most men do not like such times, but the ambitious do, the "great eagles" whom Abraham Lincoln warned his contemporaries would arise when the mob had destroyed the rule of law.[1] Such men can be saviors, or they can be mortally dangerous to public good and private liberty.

In Act 1 of *Julius Caesar*, Caesar himself points out the dangerous man in this play with lines frequently quoted: "Yond Cassius has a lean and hungry look; / He thinks too much. Such men are dangerous" (1.2.194–95).[2] Caesar never looks so

---

[1] See "The Perpetuation of Our Political Institutions: Address before the Young Men's Lyceum of Springfield, Illinois", January 27, 1838, Abraham Lincoln Online (http://showcase.netins.net/web/creative/lincoln/speeches/lyceum.htm).

[2] All quotations from *Julius Caesar* are from the edition published by Ignatius Press: *Julius Caesar*, ed. Joseph Pearce, Ignatius Critical Editions (San Francisco: Ignatius Press, 2012).

perceptive in Shakespeare's play as at this moment, when the audience has just heard Cassius berate him to Brutus as a prelude to some secret action. The timing of Caesar's political insight makes him seem prescient.

Brutus has already made us somewhat ill at ease with Cassius by his distrustful response to Cassius' praise: "Into what dangers would you lead me, Cassius ... ?" (1.2.63). In fact, the word "danger" seems to hover around Cassius like a neon warning sign. Caesar calls him dangerous; Antony denies that he is dangerous; Caesar insists that men like Cassius are "very dangerous" (1.2.210). Cassius asserts to Casca that he is indifferent to danger and then lets him know of an enterprise of "honourable-dangerous consequence" (1.3.124).

A close reading of the play reveals that Cassius is indeed dangerous. Yet Shakespeare, with his vast human, political, and historical experience, presents this most dangerous of men as one of the great tragic figures in the play, and the one who most profoundly reveals the tragedy of Rome herself.

The Act of Cassius

It is hard to sympathize with Cassius. For one thing, as readers, we tend not to be interested in him. We focus on Brutus and Caesar early, and Antony becomes important later on. Cassius comes across merely as a catalyst for the action. Indeed, his first appearance in Act 1, scene 2, might seem like a temptation scene. Cassius is Brutus' serpent, beguiling him into contemplating a hideous deed, like Iago working on Othello, or the witches on Macbeth. Indeed, Cassius seems to indict himself before the audience with his soliloquy at the end of the scene:

> Well, Brutus, thou art noble; yet, I see,
> Thy honourable mettle may be wrought
> From that it is dispos'd. Therefore it is meet
> That noble minds keep ever with their likes;
> For who so firm that cannot be seduc'd?
>   (1.2.307–11)

Is Cassius revealing that he is seducing Brutus? If this impression is strong enough, then we are ready to accept Antony's judgment at the end of the play, which lumps Cassius with the envious conspirators: "All the conspirators save only [Brutus]/Did that they did in envy of great Caesar" (5.5.69–70).

Yet rarely is a character a mere instrument for Shakespeare, one introduced simply to move the plot along or to make a point or to illuminate another character. This makes acting in his plays always exciting. Every character who speaks onstage for any length of time is a study, whose motives, character, and aspirations matter as much to the author as they would to the living person himself.

Cassius is much more than a secondary character. He dominates the opening act, through his lengthy diatribe against Caesar and his unnerving soliloquy, and even more through his brazen confrontation with the "tempest dropping fire":

> [I] bar'd my bosom to the thunder-stone;
> And when the cross blue lightning seem'd to open
> The breast of heaven, I did present myself
> Even in the aim and very flash of it.
>
> (1.3.10, 49–52)

In this scene, his exultant, fiery spirit, triumphant in readiness for the great deed, soars in consonance with the fierce storm. Contrasted with Casca's superstitious terror and Cicero's spiritless and sceptical response, Cassius should command the audience's admiration in this scene. Casca is transformed by Cassius from the "blunt fellow" lamented by Brutus back to the "quick mettle" of his school days (1.2.294, 295). By the power of his own spirit, Cassius reignites "those sparks of life/That should be in a Roman" (1.3.57–58), which Casca has lost, having sublimated his disgust with the times by putting on the satirical, foppish character that Brutus disdains. The Casca who gives his hand to Cassius, who says, "... I will set this foot of mine as far/As who goes farthest" (1.3.119–20), is infinitely preferable to the semi-man who lives only to tell the "foolery" of the times (1.2.235).

We should be amazed, not only at what Cassius does here, but at his understanding of the men around him. Brutus saw with distaste the useless Casca; Cassius saw the real Roman within Casca and perceptively brought it out. In this scene, Cassius is both inspired by the storm and immediately perceptive to how he can use it to ignite Casca.

Cassius wants to have this effect on all of Rome:

>   Romans now
> Have thews and limbs like to their ancestors.
> But woe the while! our fathers' minds are dead,
> And we are govern'd with our mothers' spirits;
> Our yoke and sufferance show us womanish.
>
>   (1.3.80–84)

A feeling of superiority expressed so forcefully can be its own reward. But for Cassius it is a call to action. He will not leave Rome in such a state without a fight. So he tells Casca, "... I have mov'd already / Some certain of the noblest-minded Romans / To undergo with me an enterprise / Of honourable-dangerous consequence" (1.3.121–24). Should he become convinced that Rome cannot be saved, that she can do no more than serve as "base matter to illuminate" the one only man within her (1.3.110), then suicide will allow "Cassius from bondage [to] deliver Cassius" (1.3.90) and defeat tyranny in the only way a powerless man, but still a man, might.

All of this should make us feel that Act 1 is the "act of Cassius". He is the one great man in this scene, the mover of all, the spirit and the thought behind the great action of the play. Yet we are ill at ease. Have we shaken off Casca's fear of the divine power of the storm and the omens?

> But wherefore did you so much tempt the heavens?
> It is the part of men to fear and tremble
> When the most mighty gods by tokens send
> Such dreadful heralds to astonish us.
>
>   (1.3.53–56)

And can we admire Cassius as he brings to completion the deception necessary for his plot, instructing Cinna to place false appeals where Brutus can find them?

"The Last of the Romans"

Cassius is a man of spirit aroused by the impending death of the Roman spirit. So strong is this aspect of his character that Brutus, the last to mention the name of Cassius, eulogizes: "The last of all the Romans, fare thee well! / It is impossible that ever Rome / Should breed thy fellow" (5.3.99–101). But does Cassius deserve this epithet, or is this another instance of Brutus idealizing the world around him? Yet Brutus is not alone in his judgment; Titinius, Cassius' companion in life and death, is even more laudatory, crying out, "The sun of Rome is set. Our day is gone" (5.3.63).

What does it mean to be a Roman in this play? Before answering this question, we should ask, who cares and why? Certainly being a Roman does matter to most of the characters, who often name themselves and others as Romans. Brutus and Cassius frequently charge their fellow conspirators to be "true Romans", to act like Romans. Brutus invites them to bathe in Caesar's blood with "Stoop, Romans, stoop" (3.1.106). Brutus cuts Cassius to the core when he flings out, "I had rather be a dog and bay the moon / Than such a Roman" (4.3.27–28). Brutus moves even the mob of Rome when he challenges, "Who is here so rude that would not be a Roman?" (3.2.29–30).

For these characters, to be a Roman is the highest moral goal, the standard by which they judge their worth and that of others. They have to measure up to all the great figures who have gone before them: Lucius Brutus, who first brought liberty to Rome, of course, and Cincinnatus, the republic's George Washington figure, who, having saved Rome, renounced supreme rule in order to return to his farm; also Fabius Maximus, who held off Hannibal's invasions, and Marcellus, conqueror of Syracuse and greatest of Roman consuls. These heroes and countless others established the Roman character; their images lie deep, indelibly fixed in the souls of their descendants.[3]

Yet not all the characters think of themselves as Romans. Antony rarely mentions Rome as more than a place. In the madness and rush of Act 3, Antony wrenches our hearts with his mourning over the fall of great Caesar yet does not refer to the fall of Rome. His terrifying prophecy-vow of civil war is driven only by his love of Caesar without thought of the destruction of Rome that will thereby come. He does not praise Caesar as a true Roman, a noble Roman, the greatest Roman, but says, "Thou art the ruins of the noblest man / That ever lived in the tide of times" (3.1.257–58). In Antony's mind, Caesar transcends Rome.

And so it is for Caesar himself. Throughout his appearances in the play, Caesar expresses the new image that inspires him to greatness—that of Caesar. Caesar's own image of himself is the only measure that he has. Why should Caesar not lie? Because it does not become a Roman? No, (but as he tells Calpurnia) because it does not become Caesar: "Shall Caesar send a lie? Have I in conquest stretch'd mine arm so far, / To be afeard to tell greybeards the truth?" (2.2.65–67). Caesar cannot be measured by Rome, for in his mind he is sui generis. No other compares to him, as he so powerfully expresses immediately before his assassination:

> I could be well mov'd, if I were as you;
> If I could pray to move, prayers would move me;
> But I am constant as the northern star,
> Of whose true-fix'd and resting quality
> There is no fellow in the firmament.
>
> (3.1.58–62)

---

[3] Polybius, the great historian of the Roman Republic, tells us that Roman funerals included a procession of young men dressed and masked as their noble ancestors. "There could not easily be a more inspiring spectacle than this for a young man of noble ambitions and virtuous aspirations. For can we conceive any one to be unmoved at the sight of all the likenesses collected together of the men who have earned glory, all as it were living and breathing?" (*The "Histories" of Polybius*, trans. Evelyn S. Shuckburgh [London: Macmillan, 1889], 6.53). Aeneas is treated to a similar procession of his great progeny in the underworld (*Aeneid* 6.1000ff.).

In the course of his funeral speech, Antony not only works the crowd into a frenzy for the blood of the conspirators, but he wreaks a more permanent change in the character of Rome. Brutus had moved the crowd by expressly subordinating his personal love of Caesar to his devotion to Rome: "Not that I lov'd Caesar less, but that I lov'd Rome more" (3.2.22–23). Antony turns the crowd around, inspiring them with his personal devotion to Caesar, showing how Rome and its citizens were indebted to him: "Why, friends, you go to do you know not what./Wherein hath Caesar thus deserv'd your loves?" "Here was a Caesar! When comes such another?" (3.2.236–37, 253). Brutus loved Caesar as a person; Antony's speech anticipates the time when Rome will love Caesar as a god.

Caesarism strikes at the root of the Roman character. To be a Roman means first and foremost to be no man's slave, to be the tool of no other man's interest. Brutus, like Cassius, fears that Caesar's absolute rule will threaten this cherished liberty. But he does not understand the threat in the way Cassius does. During his soliloquy in which he commits to the conspiracy, Brutus gives as the reason to assassinate Caesar, not that he wields absolute power, but that he will likely abuse that power. For Brutus, to be a slave is to be abused by your master. Cassius is more radical: what is intolerable is simply that Caesar has the power over him, whether he abuses it or not: "I had as lief not be as live to be/In awe of such a thing as I myself" (1.2.95–96). Cassius reports several times in which Caesar's bodily weaknesses were manifest, when Cassius even had to save him. But the new regime makes Caesar "a god", "a Colossus" (1.2.116, 136)—and "Cassius is/A wretched creature, and must bend his body/If Caesar carelessly but nod on him" (1.2.116–18). The formal subservience drives Cassius to distraction. Shakespeare has already given us a taste of the pomp around Caesar, and an ominous suggestion of the subservience that Caesar's favorites will show, when Antony responds to Caesar's command: "I shall remember./When Caesar says 'Do this', it is perform'd" (1.2.9–10).

Cassius is not driven primarily by envy, as Antony would have us think, but by indignation. Aristotle explains in his treatise *On Rhetoric* (whose ideas Shakespeare would know through his own classical training) that envy and indignation are very similar: they both involve being upset at other people's prosperity. But good men get indignant when the undeserving get rewarded: "[F]or it is right to sympathize with and pity those who suffer undeservedly and to feel indignation at those who undeservedly fare well; for what takes place contrary to deserts is unjust, and thus we attribute being indignant to gods."[4] When a coward, for example, gets a medal of honor, the truly brave men will be furious. They might even go to great lengths to prevent the medal being given, or to expose the injustice afterward. Frequently, this will look like envy to those who do not know the true situation. Envy is the pain felt when someone who is our equal gets something that makes them look better than we do. "And people have envy of those who have acquired something or been successful . . . for clearly [these people] do not attain this good because of themselves, so distress at this causes envy."[5]

Is Cassius indignant or envious of Caesar? Clearly Cassius feels righteous indignation, as any real Roman would feel at a fellow being raised to the honors of a god. Does Cassius give any indication that he wishes he had the honors that have been heaped upon Caesar? That if only Cassius had worked harder, he could have been Caesar instead? Not at all. Rather, Shakespeare seems to enhance Caesar's limitations, even including a gratuitous reference to his deaf ear, in order to excite our indignation in sympathy with Cassius.

Cassius sees more than the injustice of Caesar's elevation; he sees that Caesar's height demands the debasement of everyone else. Cassius faces the problem of kingship rather than that of tyranny. As Aristotle points out in his *Politics*, absolute kingship is proper only when the king is of a different order of

---

[4] Aristotle, *On Rhetoric: A Theory of Political Discourse*, trans. George A. Kennedy (New York: Oxford University Press, 1991), 2.9.2.

[5] Ibid., 2.10.7.

being from his subjects.[6] He is as father and shepherd to his people, which implies that they are his children and sheep and not grown men at all. In fact, since all rule and decision belong to the one man, the chance to engage in political prudence and governance is denied to anyone else. From this viewpoint, Cassius stirs Brutus by putting the case against kingship to him:

> When could they say, till now, that talk'd of Rome,
> That her wide walls encompass'd but one man?
> Now is it Rome indeed, and room enough,
> When there is in it but one only man.
>
> (1.2.154–57)

As long as Romans were free and equal, the glory of Rome belonged to all. If you lived up to your Roman character and your devotion to Rome, the glory of Rome belonged to you. You ruled the earth as a Roman. In the new order, the glory of Rome belongs to one only man in Rome, Caesar. Others can share in that only insofar as they make themselves limbs of Caesar.

Does a Roman accept subservience as long as the master is benevolent? Antony has no problem with this, nor does Brutus—at least as far as his soliloquy reveals. Brutus has fared well by Caesar; he has been honored by him and has been admitted among his friends. If he could trust that Caesar would continue to do well by him and by all, then well and good. Only because he is convinced that Caesar will succumb to the temptations of power does he believe the assassination to be justified. And so, explicitly rejecting Cassius' complaint, Brutus soliloquizes:

> And since the quarrel
> Will bear no colour for the thing he is,
> Fashion it thus—that what he is, augmented,
> Would run to these and these extremities ....
>
> (2.1.28–31)

---

[6] See, for example, *Politics* 1.12.1259b10–17, 3.13.1284a3–23.

Cassius grasps exactly what is at stake: the very Roman character. Caesar confirms this in his aside to Antony in Act 1. Caesar wants "fat" men around him (1.2.192), ones who enjoy their food and want to look good, who revel in the theater and music. Cassius is a threat because he studies men and understands their motives and what they are up to: "He reads much,/He is a great observer, and he looks/ Quite through the deeds of men" (1.2.201–3). Caesar needs fawners like Antony, whose glory is to be a limb of Caesar, not men like Cassius who think their own thoughts and insist on judging for themselves. Cassius recognizes that living as the only man in Rome, as one like a god, has taken away Caesar's own humanity: "Poor man! I know he would not be a wolf/But that he sees the Romans are but sheep" (1.3.104–5).

We are now in a position to understand Cassius' "seduction" soliloquy. Aroused by the threat to the Roman ideal, the ideal under which he judges himself, Cassius has been driven to the desperate step of an assassination conspiracy. He seeks only noble Romans to join. But is Brutus noble? Brutus would be so tremendously helpful to the success of the conspiracy. But does Brutus care? Brutus is a friend of Caesar; is he another Antony? Is that why Brutus has stopped showing signs of friendship to Cassius? In their dialogue in Act 1, Cassius is not simply trying to win Brutus to the conspiracy; he is testing his Roman spirit. He is encouraged that Brutus is deeply troubled at the thought that Caesar might be made king. But Cassius worries that Caesar's honors may win over the heart of Brutus and his loyalty.

> Well, Brutus, thou art noble; yet I see,
> Thy honourable mettle may be wrought
> From that it is dispos'd. Therefore it is meet
> That noble minds keep ever with their likes;
> For who so firm that cannot be seduc'd?
>   (1.2.307–11)

Roman Friend

Cassius' devotion to Brutus also shows him to be a true Roman. Romans valued friendship as much as the spirit of freedom. "Friend" as noun and "love" as verb abound throughout the play. A Roman is a man worthy of friendship, one with many noble friends who will stick by him through thick and thin and who can rely completely on him in return. Male friendship plays as prominent a role in *Julius Caesar*, as in any other play of Shakespeare. Artemidorus signs his letter to Caesar, "Thy lover" (2.3.6). Brutus' funeral oration, which begins, "Romans, countrymen, and lovers" (3.2.13), is full of claims that he loved Caesar. Even Caesar wants to play at friendship: "Good friends, go in and taste some wine with me; / And we, like friends, will straightway go together" (2.2.125–26). Friendship and love are at the center of the action and passion of this play: Brutus and Caesar, Antony and Caesar, and above all, Cassius and Brutus.

Cassius first comes to our attention as an uncertain friend, inviting Brutus to come watch the race with him. When Brutus refuses, Cassius asks what is wrong, for Brutus has grown distant from him. Cassius' passion in Act 4 reveals that in this first encounter, Cassius is not only wondering about Brutus' attachment to Caesar but is also hurt at the withdrawing of friendship by another whom he admires. Cassius' personal attachment to Brutus cannot be underestimated or overplayed. In all the actions of the play, when Cassius sees the way that will lead to success, he defers to Brutus against his own better judgment. Cassius needs Brutus' support, perhaps more personally than politically.

Cassius' devotion to Brutus, and his vulnerability, appear full force in Act 4. This entire scene deserves a book, but a short treatment will begin to illumine Cassius the friend. Cassius and Brutus are both angry at each other, and both have deeper, personal reasons for their anger than the political slights they believe they have suffered. Brutus, as we learn later, has just been informed of his wife's death. But Cassius is afflicted above all by Brutus' indifference to him and is driven mad by Brutus' evident desire to hurt him: "Strike as thou didst at Caesar; for I know,/When thou didst hate him worst, thou lov'dst him better/Than ever thou lov'dst Cassius" (4.3.103–5). Cassius repeatedly wonders that he allows Brutus to insult him; only his deep love, respect, and psychological need of Brutus' love can explain it. Brutus takes advantage of this to drive a dagger deep into Cassius' heart.

The depths of Cassius' love for Brutus in the end save their friendship. In this scene, Shakespeare brings the audience to the verge of the catastrophe that seems the appropriate fate of all conspirators—they turn viciously on each other and so seem about to do most of the dirty work for their enemies. But Cassius' endurance, his admission of fault, his plea for indulgence, and finally his literal offer of his heart on a dagger break through Brutus' spiteful anger. This crisis, instead of destroying their friendship along with their hope of defeating Antony and Octavius, actually deepens their friendship through bearing with each other, through compassion and forgiveness.

> *Brutus.*   Give me a bowl of wine.
>   In this I bury all unkindness, Cassius.
> *Cassius.* My heart is thirsty for that noble pledge.
>   Fill, Lucius, till the wine o'erswell the cup;
>   I cannot drink too much of Brutus' love. (4.3.156–60)

Duplicity and Unbelief

In his devotion to Roman character, his indignation at monarchy, and his passionate friendship, Cassius shows himself a true Roman. But, driven by the times, he falls short of the Roman character in two important ways. Honesty is the mark of Roman character most prized by Brutus. When Cassius would have the conspirators swear an oath, Brutus forcefully replies that

                    every drop of blood
That every Roman bears, and nobly bears,
Is guilty of a several bastardy,
If he do break the smallest particle
Of any promise that hath pass'd from him.
                              (2.1.136–40)

In the opening act, Cassius asserts that Brutus knows Cassius is not a man accustomed to dissimulation or manipulation. In the rest of that conversation with Brutus, he expresses vehemently exactly what he thinks of Caesar. Before he spoke, Cassius needed to know that Brutus was his friend and that he was disturbed by Caesar's ascendancy, but once assured, he completely unburdened his mind and heart before Brutus.

And yet Cassius deceives Brutus with planted notes. In fact, the entire conspiracy is antithetical to the Roman character. Fidelity among the conspirators is assumed, yet Brutus immediately enjoins them to put on their parts "as our Roman actors do" (2.1.226). Conspiracy and duplicity go hand in hand. How Shakespeare expects us to view the assassination may be unclear, but the falseness assumed by the conspirators puts a cloud over the whole business. Ever practical, Cassius, believing in the necessity of such duplicity (as he does the necessity of the political murder of men like Antony and the use of bribes in running a successful war), enters into it without regret. Yet this aspect, the duplicity, makes us sympathetic to Antony's accusation in the prebattle confrontation at Philippi:

        Villains, you did not so when your vile
          daggers
        Hack'd one another in the sides of Caesar.
        You show'd your teeth like apes, and fawn'd like
          hounds,
        And bow'd like bondmen, kissing Caesar's feet;
        Whilst damned Casca, like a cur, behind
        Struck Caesar on the neck. O you flatterers!
                              (5.1.39–44)

Should the supposed political necessity of removing Caesar, an action necessary to save the Roman character, lead Cassius, Brutus, and the rest to such a betrayal? Antony, who knows how to drive the feelings of the crowd, here sways the audience to blame the conspirators.

Cassius believes in his own personal honesty and that of the Roman character, though he also believes that the need of the time justifies honesty's temporary neglect. But in the matter of omens, of divine intervention generally, Cassius has completely turned his back on ancient Roman belief through a nontraditional Roman pastime, philosophy. Cassius explains late in the play that he had been a follower of Epicurus. Epicurus taught that the gods, happy in themselves, have no interest in the affairs of men. Coupled with an atom-based doctrine that the soul dies with the body, Epicureanism freed men from fears of the gods and the afterlife. This philosophy leaves Cassius free to act without fear. The stars do not govern us, nor do the gods send us signs; we can make of ourselves what we will: "Men at some time are masters of their fates;/The fault, dear Brutus, is not in our stars,/But in ourselves, that we are underlings" (1.2.139–40). He does not shudder, as Casca does, at the fearful storm on the eve of the deadly act. Yet the audience does. Throughout the first three acts, the numinous aspects of life that are beyond our power bring warning after warning against the act. Signs and wonders in the night, prophets, dreams all warn Caesar to stay home on the ides of March. The gods, the providential powers who never show their faces (if they have them), do not want Caesar to die, and Plutarch, Shakespeare's main source for the entire story, suggests a reason: "[I]n the malady of the times and the need of a monarchical government, [Caesar] might be thought to have been sent as the gentlest physician, by no other than a divine intervention."[7]

---

[7] *Plutarch's "Lives": The Dryden Translation*, ed. Arthur Hugh Clough (New York: Modern Library, 2001), pp. 609–10.

At the heart of the tragedy of Cassius is that his philosophy, and perhaps his spirit, refuses to recognize, to look for, signs of divine providence. Confident in himself and his judgments, he takes it upon himself to rid himself and Rome of what he considers an unbearable evil. The ancient Romans, militarily aggressive and confident though they were, never went into battle without consulting the omens. If a slaughtered chicken's liver was too yellow, if a flock of vultures flew north to south, an entire army, ready for victory, would not march—not so much because they might fail, but because, win or lose, they would displease the gods. As Christians, we might smile at the superstition, yet we should applaud the desire. Romans never trusted their own judgment in acts of great importance and sought through the only means they had to know the will of the gods.

In turning his back on this ancient practice, in denying in principle that the gods exercise any providential concern for the affairs of men, Cassius has abandoned the religious core that tamed the Roman military character and lifted the Romans above the ruthless, savage outlaws who gathered around Romulus to found the city. Numa, king after Romulus, introduced religion (and law along with it) into Roman society. Cassius embarks on his great enterprise without any attempt to consult the will of the gods. Late in the play, he begins to recognize his misjudgment: "You know that I held Epicurus strong,/ And his opinion; now I change my mind,/ And partly credit things that do presage" (5.1.76–78).

The Tragedy of Cassius

Too late this partial conversion, and too partial perhaps. Cassius tells Messala privately that the auspices he would now believe are against their army. A Roman, in the face of the inauspicious, would refrain from the action, which in this case might mean Cassius would have to surrender. Yet, "fresh of spirit and resolv'd", he lies to Brutus, "Now, most noble Brutus,/ The gods to-day stand friendly, that we may,/ Lovers in peace, lead on our days to age!" (5.1.90, 93–94). And so we come to the tragic culmination of the play. The battle, the futile slaughter of the last of the noble Romans, occurs. Cassius, perhaps led on by the omens he believed in but refused to obey, takes his life when victory is in his grasp. And in his fall, he also shows that his tragedy is the tragedy of Rome herself.

For a Roman, suicide is the only way out finally from an intolerable situation brought about by a catastrophic failure. Brutus will join Cassius in this end, though Brutus knows better. In the final meeting of the great friends, Brutus shows that he has in his understanding reached beyond the Roman character. Suicide, the Roman way, is "cowardly" (5.1.103). Brutus has believed this all his adult life. His Stoic philosophy, unlike Cassius' Epicureanism, held strongly that the whole course of human and natural affairs witnessed a wise providence. So Stoicism taught submission to all the seeming evils that threaten to poison our lives. Because of this, Brutus always blamed Cato, the quintessential model of Roman fortitude, who took his life rather than submit himself to Caesar. Cato should have known, as Brutus knew, that a man should arm himself "with patience / To stay [await] the providence of some high powers / That govern us below" (5.1.105–7).

Yet Cassius, the Roman in spirit, challenges Brutus even in the end. And Brutus chooses the Roman way, the Roman spirit, over the philosophy that counsels submission to Providence.

> *Cassius.*   Then, if we lose this battle,
>   You are contented to be led in triumph
>   Through the streets of Rome?
> *Brutus.* No, Cassius, no. Think not, thou noble Roman,
>   That ever Brutus will go bound to Rome;
>   He bears too great a mind. (5.1.107–12)

The tragedy of Cassius is complete, bitter, overwhelming. In him, the noble Roman spirit, excusing dishonesty and neglecting the gods, brings down not only himself but his dear, most admired, and noble friend, and thousands of his compatriots, failing to save himself and Rome, succeeding only in setting loose the dogs of war.

The twentieth century witnessed many such Machiavellian tragedies, as a passionate hatred of injustice burst forth from the constraints of honesty and religion to bring about civil wars, world wars, and social destruction. In this new century, as lust for pleasure undermines Western character and lust for power grows more brazen in acquisition and exercise, men and women of spirit, full of indignation at the great evils around them, will be passionately urged from within to do whatever it takes to make things right. The lesson of *Julius Caesar* is to consult Providence and the signs of the times: these might urge submitting to evil and enduring with trust in that Providence, rather than the manly action so natural to the human spirit.

Bibliography

Aristotle. *On Rhetoric: A Theory of Political Discourse*. Translated by George A. Kennedy. New York: Oxford University Press, 1991.

Aristotle. *The Politics*. Translated by Carnes Lord. Chicago: University of Chicago Press, 1984.

Plutarch. *Plutarch's "Lives": The Dryden Translation*. Edited by Arthur Hugh Clough. New York: Modern Library, 2001.

Polybius. *The "Histories" of Polybius*. Translated by Evelyn S. Shuckburgh. London: Macmillan, 1889.

Shakespeare, William. *Julius Caesar*. Edited by Joseph Pearce. Ignatius Critical Editions. San Francisco: Ignatius Press, 2012.

Virgil. *The "Aeneid" of Virgil*. Translated by Allen Mandelbaum. Berkeley: University of California Press, 1964.

CONTRIBUTORS

James Bemis is an editorial board member, weekly columnist, and film critic for *California Political Review* and is a frequent contributor to the *Latin Mass* magazine. His five-part series "Through the Eyes of the Church", on the Vatican's list of the forty-five "Most Important Films in the Century of Cinema", was published in the *Wanderer*. His essays on film adaptations of *Romeo and Juliet*, *King Lear*, *The Merchant of Venice*, and *Macbeth* have appeared in the Ignatius Critical Editions of these four plays.

Michael Hanke obtained his Ph.D. in 1993 and his habilitation in 2003. He has lectured and taught at German universities and has published books on John Crowe Ransom, Roy Campbell, and German Expressionist poetry, and articles on Renaissance, nineteenth-century, and twentieth-century English literature. He has also edited several collections of critical essays.

James E. Hartley is professor of economics at Mount Holyoke College, where he teaches courses on macroeconomics and money and banking, as well as interdisciplinary courses on Western civilization. He has served as the director of the first-year seminar program at Mount Holyoke and was a Fulbright scholar in India.

Sophia Mason is a northern Virginia freelance writer, a Thomas Aquinas College graduate, and the oldest of ten children. Her work has appeared in the *Saint Austin Review* and the *Arlington Catholic Herald*. Her weaknesses (besides Shakespeare) include long Victorian novels, fantasies, and detective stories. She blogs as The Girl Who Was Saturday (http://girlwhowassaturday.blogspot.com/).

Susan Vandiver Nicassio is professor of history at the University of Louisiana at Lafayette and is the author of several books, including *Tosca's Rome* (University of Chicago Press, 2000) and *Rome Under Napoleon* (University of Chicago Press, 2009). A reformed opera singer, she is a Fulbright scholar and a Fellow of the American Academy in Rome.

Joseph Pearce is writer in residence and associate professor of literature at Ave Maria University in Florida. He is the author of *The Quest for Shakespeare* (Ignatius Press, 2008) and *Through Shakespeare's Eyes* (Ignatius Press, 2010) and has hosted two thirteen-part television series on Shakespeare for EWTN. He has edited the Ignatius Critical Editions of *King Lear*, *Hamlet*, *The Merchant of Venice*, *Macbeth*, and *Romeo and Juliet* and is coeditor of the *Saint Austin Review* (www.staustinreview.com).

Andrew T. Seeley (Medieval Studies, University of Toronto) has been a tutor at Thomas Aquinas College in California since 1992 and director of the Institute for Catholic Liberal Education since 2005. He is coauthor of *Declaration Statesmanship: A Course in American Government* and has directed several amateur Shakespeare productions.